The Compassionate Diet®

HOW WHAT YOU EAT
CAN CHANGE YOUR LIFE AND
SAVE THE PLANET

The
Compassionate
Diet®

ARRAN STEPHENS

with

ELIOT JAY ROSEN

RODALE

© 2011 by Arran Stephens

All rights reserved. No part of this publication may be reproduced or transmitted in any form or by any means, electronic or mechanical, including photocopying, recording, or any other information storage and retrieval system, without the written permission of the publisher.

Rodale books may be purchased for business or promotional use or for special sales. For information, please write to: Special Markets Department, Rodale Inc., 733 Third Avenue, New York, NY 10017.

Printed in the United States of America
Rodale Inc. makes every effort to use acid-free ♾, recycled paper ♲.

Book design by Elizabeth Van Itallie
Illustrations by Melanie Marder Parks

Library of Congress Cataloging-in-Publication Data
Stephens, Arran.
 The compassionate diet : how what you eat can change your life and save the planet / Arran Stephens with Elliot Jay Rosen.
  p.   cm.
 Includes bibliographical references and index.
 ISBN 978-1-60961-063-0 (pbk)
 1. Vegetarianism.   I. Rosen, Eliot Jay.   II. Title.
 TX392.S735   2011
 613.2'62—dc22   2010047761

Distributed to the trade by Macmillan
2   4   6   8   10   9   7   5   3   1   paperback

To Life, Light & Service

Contents

Vegetarianism and Longevity: The Evidence •
Famous Vegetarians • African American Vegetarians
• Amerindian Vegetarians • The Dangers of Animal
Food Consumption

Dispelling Lingering Myths • Getting Enough
Protein • Getting Enough Calcium • Getting Enough
Vitamin B_{12} • Human Physiology: Is It Wise to Eat
Meat? • Formal Studies • Official Recognition by
Health Authorities • The Vegetarian Food Pyramid

Foreword

Today, the vegetarian diet is popular for its health benefits, its innate compassion toward animals, and its ecological responsibility. In the last few decades, the wellness-enhancing aspect of this diet has been scientifically proven.

Yet beyond health, ethical, or ecological considerations, there is a fundamental spiritual aspect to the vegetarian diet. For an ever-growing number of people, choosing to be a vegetarian has also been a conscious decision to enhance their inner spiritual lives.

Since ancient times, vegetarianism has been associated with a life of nonviolence and love toward all of God's creatures. Many saints and seers from diverse religious traditions have followed a vegetarian diet. In fact, the vegetarian diet is considered so important in the Sant Mat tradition that its spiritual masters reveal the sacred initiation (meditation) instructions only to those who follow a vegetarian diet. In *The Compassionate Diet*, a compelling case is made for becoming a vegetarian. Vegetarianism is good for our health, it reduces the risk of disease, it is ecologically and economically beneficial for people around the world, and it is ecologically beneficial for our planet. Whether you decide to pursue the vegetarian diet for purely spiritual reasons or because of physical, ethical, or ecological reasons, in this book you will find information and resources presented in a clear and easy-to-understand manner.

It is my hope that readers of this book discover why vegetarianism is a gift for body, mind, and soul.

—RAJINDER SINGH

EDITOR'S NOTE: Sant Rajinder Singh Ji Maharaj is a renowned spiritual luminary and the head of Science of Spirituality, a nonprofit, nonsectarian organization with more than 1,000 centers throughout the world. His books, *Empowering Your Soul through Meditation, Spiritual Pearls for Enlightened Living, Inner and Outer Peace through Meditation* (with a foreword by H.H. the Dalai Lama), and *Silken Thread of the Divine*, have brought peace, wisdom, and guidance to countless people in many countries and cultures. He teaches meditation on the inner light and sound current inherent within all, free of charge.

For more information, visit the Web site of Science of Spirituality at www.sos.org.

> CHILDREN WHO GROW UP GETTING NUTRITION FROM PLANT FOODS RATHER THAN MEATS HAVE A TREMENDOUS HEALTH ADVANTAGE. THEY ARE LESS LIKELY TO DEVELOP WEIGHT PROBLEMS, DIABETES, HIGH BLOOD PRESSURE AND SOME FORMS OF CANCER.
> —BENJAMIN SPOCK, MD

Acknowledgments

The Compassionate Diet began after the 1999 publication of my first book, *Journey to the Luminous: Encounters with Mystic Adepts of Our Century.* The subject of diet had been only superficially addressed in my book, yet it was so integral to the transformational quest. I felt the need to write an in-depth piece on diet, grounded in the heart of compassion yet supported by important recent scientific, environmental, social, and historical research. Of special interest to me was the almost universal embracing of compassion for animals by most of the founders and philosophers of the world's great spiritual traditions. Why yet another book on this topic? Hopefully to inspire others to consider a win-win life and a planet-changing shift.

I would like to thank those who have worked with me on this project: Eliot Rosen, who, several years into the project, was invited to participate and contribute his excellent research, writing skills, and insights; author/friend John Robbins for his suggestions and quotations; and my life companion, Ratana, for her patience and love. Last but not least, I am most grateful to the renowned spiritual leader and meditation master H.H. Sant Rajinder Singh Ji Maharaj, who agreed, to my surprise and delight, when I hesitantly asked if he would consider writing the foreword to this little book. His memorable and elegant message is a gift that speaks for itself.

—ARRAN STEPHENS

Preface

At the outset—and with deepest respect—I should say that my views are based upon a life of personal dietary experiment, observation, and research, and are not meant as judgments against anyone for his or her particular choices or beliefs.

What I call "the compassionate diet" is an opportunity to actualize a more humane, peaceful lifestyle that honors the myriad sentient beings that share our unique planet. Like us, they too wish to live out their natural life spans.

When I discontinued eating meat, fish, fowl, and eggs at the age of twenty in 1964, my primary motivation was a deepening love and respect for all living creatures. This commitment, which has been joyfully kept, was one of the easiest I have ever made, and involved very little sense of self-denial. The invigorating effects were soon felt and the heart's inherent capacity for compassion expanded; I began to experience animals as younger relatives in a universal family of conscious beings. This understanding was deeply instinctive and intuitive.

The most immediate personal benefit of adopting a compassionate diet was a great increase in physical energy. My youthful vitality, squandered during five years of dissolute living and poor food choices, was remarkably restored. One week after embracing a vegetarian lifestyle, my truth quest led me to the great luminary H.H. Sant Kirpal Singh Ji Maharaj (1894–1974) and the inner spiritual science he imparted. The dietary transition supported my meditative journey, and greatly enhanced my soul's ability to take flight. This new lifestyle gave me the physical energy to make the change I wanted to see and become.

As an active participant in the holistic health movement for four and a half decades, I've witnessed many dietary fads come and go, but a balanced and natural vegetarian diet is neither a fad nor a passing trend. It has been part of many cultures over untold millennia. In 1969, I was pleased to learn that my Indian bride, Ratana, and her family had been lacto-vegetarians for many generations. Our four children and grandchildren, born and raised in the West, have all enjoyed the health and spiritual benefits of a completely meatless diet—including no chicken, fish, or eggs.

Globally, we feed 756 million tons of grain to farmed animals per year. As Princeton bioethicist Peter Singer notes, if we fed that grain to the 1.4 billion people who are living in abject poverty, each of them would be provided with more than half a ton of grain, or about three pounds of grain per day—that's twice the amount they would need to survive. And that doesn't even include the 225 million tons of soy that is produced every year, almost all of which is fed to farmed animals. He writes, "The world is not running out of food. The problem is that we, the relatively affluent, have found a way to consume four or five times as much food as would be possible, if we were to eat the crops we grow directly."

My wife and I attended the Fortune Green Conference in 2008, and we heard presentations from the CEOs of many Fortune 500 companies. At this prestigious "green" conference, major corporations proudly reported significant strides in reducing their carbon footprints. While any reduction in carbon pollution is laudable, none of these companies made any connection between the profoundly negative effects of animal foods and chemical agriculture on global warming

If everyone became a vegetarian for just one day, the United States would save:

- *100 billion gallons of water*
- *1.5 billion pounds of crops otherwise fed to livestock*
- *70 million gallons of gas—enough to fuel all the cars of Canada and Mexico, with plenty to spare*
- *3 million acres of land*
- *33 tons of antibiotics*
- *Greenhouse gas emissions equal to 1.2 million tons of carbon dioxide—as much as produced by all of France*
- *3 million tons of soil erosion and $70 million in resulting economic damages*
- *4.5 million tons of animal excrement*
- *Almost 7 tons of ammonia emissions, a major air pollutant*

According to Environmental Defense, if every American skipped one meal of chicken per week and substituted vegetarian foods instead, the carbon dioxide savings would be the same as taking more than 500,000 cars off US roads.

and worldwide environmental destruction. Furthermore, nothing was said about the risks associated with genetically engineered (GE) crops and their inability to increase yields, according to a landmark 2008 study comparing GE and non-GE corn and soy.

The pages that follow aspire to deepen the reader's appreciation of the numerous spiritual, ecological, health, and economic benefits of choosing the vegetarian way of life. I wish to again thank my good friend Eliot Rosen—a dedicated health writer and author—who has provided invaluable insight and commentary throughout this collaborative process.

—ARRAN STEPHENS

Introduction

What we eat is of such importance to human progress and health, ecological balance, and animal welfare that food, like politics and religion, has become a highly charged and controversial issue. While diet is important, it is equally so not to injure the feelings and beliefs of others. Mutual respect is therefore highly valued and necessary, while holding fast to one's ideals.

Over the millennia of recorded history, and to this present day, philosophers, scientists, ethicists, sages, and seers have weighed in on the issue of vegetarianism. Research has brought to light many startling and eloquent testimonies that join with numerous recent scientific studies to build an extraordinarily strong case. The vegetarian way of life is truly a diet for all reasons.

FOR HEALTH

Millions worldwide make the change to a vegetarian diet to improve their health. Fruits, vegetables, grains, beans, nuts, seeds, seaweeds, and other plant foods contain vital elements not found in animal flesh. The health risks associated with animal foods are now indisputable. There is a direct correlation between the amount of animal foods consumed and the incidence of degenerative disease.

FOR THE ENVIRONMENT

The destruction of ancient rain forests, loss of topsoil, massive increases in water impurities, and copious amounts of carbon dioxide and other greenhouse gas pollution result from the raising of animals for food. Vegetarianism is kinder to the earth and offers hope for saving the 60 million people who die of starvation each year—15 million of them children. If the grain used to fatten livestock were fed to humans, starvation could be completely averted—not to speak of the folly of growing corn to fuel cars.

FOR THE ETHICAL ISSUE OF ANIMAL WELFARE

In factory farm settings, billions of animals are killed for food each year in the United States alone. The quote that follows, from People for the Ethical Treatment of Animals (PETA), describes the cruel torture these sentient beings experience.

> Factory-farm animals are treated like meat, milk, and egg machines. Chickens have their sensitive beaks seared off with a hot blade, and male cattle and pigs are castrated without any painkillers. All farmed chickens, turkeys and pigs spend their brief lives in dark and crowded warehouses, many of them so cramped that they can't even turn around or spread a single wing.

They are mired in their own waste, and the stench of ammonia fills the air. Animals raised for food are bred and drugged to grow as large as possible as quickly as possible—many are so heavy that they become crippled under their own weight and die within inches of their water supply.

Animals on factory farms do not see the sun or get a breath of fresh air until they are prodded and crammed onto trucks for a nightmarish ride to the slaughter-house, often through weather extremes and always without food or water. Many die during transport, and others are too sick or weak to walk off the truck after they reach the slaughterhouse.

The animals that survive this hellish ordeal are hung upside-down and their throats are slit, often while they're completely conscious. Many are still alive while they are skinned, hacked into pieces, or scalded in the defeathering tanks.

By switching to a vegetarian diet, you save more than 100 animals a year from this misery.

—PETA

We recommend watching *The Meatrix*, an animated film posted at www.themeatrix.com, for an entertaining but serious look at factory farms.

FOR SPIRITUAL LIFE

Vegetarianism, like ethical living in general, is foundational to spiritual growth and the development of universal consciousness and love. According to many of the world's wisdom traditions, meat eating is antithetical to achieving these states of expanded awareness.

In some of these ancient spiritual traditions, vegetarianism is unequivocally advocated, yet it is a sad fact that many modern-day exponents either have forgotten or deny the original teachings. Examples are the utterances of Siddhartha Gautama—the Buddha—that were written down in the Pali language by his direct disciples; several Judeo-Christian texts, written in Aramaic, that were excluded from what became the King James Version of the Christian Bible; various esoteric Taoist teachings; and the writings and living guidance of spiritually realized human beings variously called masters, saints, prophets, and sages. Many diverse traditions caution that our full human/divine potential cannot be realized if we indulge in animal foods.

Sparing life through dietary choice is an act of compassion by and for the individual person, as well as for mammals, birds, fish, and other animals used for food; in actuality, it is having compassion for one's own self! Many teachers and traditions indicate that the eating of animal foods carries heavy karmic penalties. It may be every soul's ultimate urge to reunite with its Source, but according to many great spiritual traditions, meat eating delays the process.

A well-balanced vegetarian diet is also conducive to the practice of meditation. If the body is the temple of God, pure vegetarian food, obtained honestly and eaten in moderation, helps maintain excellent health while improving one's powers of concentration. Concentration is crucial not just for meditation, but for success in any endeavor, whether spiritual, academic, scientific, artistic, or professional.

> Compassion for animals is intimately connected with goodness of character, and it may confidently be asserted that he who is cruel to animals cannot be a good man.
>
> —ARTHUR SCHOPENHAUER

When we lead a vegetarian way of life, our body is nourished by foods that keep us stable and healthy. Then, our chances of recognizing who we are—by a process of self-realization and connecting with God—are increased. We should look not only at the physical benefits of the vegetarian diet but realize that the connection with our true self is enhanced tremendously. We will then be able to fulfill the very purpose for which we came into this world.

—SANT RAJINDER SINGH

1.
What Is a Vegetarian?

_____

By definition, a vegetarian doesn't eat the flesh, blood, or body parts, in any form or quantity, of any mammals (cows, sheep, pigs, deer, antelope, etc.); or any fish (including lobsters and shellfish, etc.); any birds (chickens, turkeys, and other fowl); or any eggs, fertile or infertile, which are the embryos of unborn birds or fish.

Some people consider themselves vegetarian if they abstain from red meat but continue to eat other flesh foods; however, by the universally accepted definition of vegetarianism, this a misnomer. To call oneself a pesca- (fish) vegetarian or ovo- (egg) vegetarian is a contradiction in terms.

A celebrated poet-saint of the twentieth century, Sant Darshan Singh Ji Maharaj, said in "The Vegetarian Way of Life":

> I am often asked about the rationale of not taking
> even infertile eggs, which some people even label as
> "vegetarian eggs." Apart from the fact that such an egg
> represents a form of life which cannot fulfill itself, it
> has the same undesirable effect on us as a fertile egg. It
> stupefies the mind and enflames the passions. Taking

these factors into view, the saints and sages from time immemorial have followed the pure diet because it is most helpful for spiritual advancement.

A lacto-vegetarian diet includes animal by-products such as dairy and honey because these do not directly lead to loss of life, as the eating of animal products themselves does. A vegan—also called a strict vegetarian—abstains from all animal by-products.

> WHEN WE KILL THE ANIMALS TO EAT THEM, THEY END UP KILLING US BECAUSE THEIR FLESH, WHICH CONTAINS CHOLESTEROL AND SATURATED FAT, WAS NEVER INTENDED FOR HUMAN BEINGS.
> —WILLIAM C. ROBERTS, MD, EDITOR, *AMERICAN JOURNAL OF CARDIOLOGY*

Vegetarianism and Longevity: The Evidence

M any large population studies have found that vegetarians and vegans live longer than meat eaters: According to a Loma Linda University study, vegetarians live about seven years longer and vegans about fifteen years longer than meat eaters. The Cornell-China-Oxford Project on Nutrition, Environment and Health, conducted by Cornell University, Oxford University, and Chinese researchers—to date the largest population study on the relationship of diet to health—found that those Chinese who ate the least amount of animal products had correspondingly lower risks of cancer, heart attacks, and other chronic degenerative diseases. A British study tracked 6,000 vegetarians and 5,000 meat eaters for twelve years and found that vegetarians were 40 percent less likely to die from cancer during that time and 20 percent less likely to die from other diseases.

Every once in a while we read in the newspaper about an active centenarian dying peacefully in his or her sleep despite having, for the last eighty years, smoked, drunk alcohol, and eaten meat. These people are genetic superstars who were able to mistreat their bodies with health-robbing substances and still live a long time by virtue of the strength of their genetic inheritance. Who knows how much longer they might have lived, or how much better the quality of life they might have enjoyed, had they eaten lower on the food chain—specifically, a plant-based diet. Emulate their lifestyle at your peril!

The twentieth-century playwright George Bernard Shaw waxed ironic:

> The average age (longevity) of a meat eater is 63. I am on the verge of 85 and still work as hard as ever. I have lived quite long enough and am trying to die; but I simply cannot do it. A single beef-steak would finish me; but I cannot bring myself to swallow it. I am oppressed with a dread of living forever. That is the only disadvantage of vegetarianism.

Famous Vegetarians

The list of illustrious vegetarians continues to grow. There are now several "big lists" of famous vegetarians on the Internet. One particularly good one is available at www.ivu.org/people, on the Web site of the International Vegetarian Union. While *who* is on such a list isn't so important, the sheer number of amazingly diverse and talented individuals is impressive. To mention a few examples from the twentieth century: Clara Barton (founder of the American Red Cross), writer Leo Tolstoy, General William Booth (founder of the Salvation Army), Mahatma Gandhi, and auto magnate Henry Ford were all conscientious longtime vegetarians. When told by his doctors in his ninetieth year that he would have to begin to eat meat to survive, George Bernard Shaw responded with his characteristic humor:

> I solemnly declare that it is my last wish that when I am no longer a captive of this physical body, that my coffin when carried to the graveyard be accompanied

by mourners of the following categories: first, birds; second, sheep, lambs, cows and other animals of the kind; third, live fish in an aquarium. Each of these mourners should carry a placard bearing the inscription: "O Lord, be gracious to our benefactor G.B. Shaw who gave his life for saving ours!"

Clearly, vegetarianism has been no bar to greatness in any walk of life. Leonardo da Vinci, the Renaissance genius, was even more outspoken about the brutality of meat eating:

Truly man is the king of beasts, for his brutality exceeds them. We live by the death of others. [Our bodies] are burial places! I have since an early age abjured the use of meat, and the time will come when men will look upon the murder of animals as they now look upon the murder of men.

Leonardo often bought captive birds from the market and set them free from their cages. He was so strong that he could bend a gold florin between his thumb and forefinger, and when confronted by Michelangelo about his so-called effete lifestyle, Leonardo bent a thick iron bar with his bare hands and tossed it to the jealous Michelangelo. It was perhaps Leonardo's vegetarian diet that helped him live nearly twice as long as average Europeans of his time.

The great mathematician and spiritual master Pythagoras was a strict vegetarian who required his disciples to be vegetarians as well. In fact, for centuries in Europe, vegetarians were called "Pythagoreans."

One of the greatest modern theoretical physicists, Edward Witten, PhD, developer of superstring theory, is a vegetarian. Another famous physicist, Albert Einstein, a vegetarian sympathizer for decades, finally became a vegetarian later in life. In a letter to Max Kariel, he said, "I have always eaten animal flesh with a somewhat guilty conscience." And in another letter, to his friend Hans Muehsam: "So I am [now] living . . . without meat, without fish, but am feeling quite well this way," he wrote. "It always seems to me that man was not born to be a carnivore."

Einstein also wrote:

> Besides agreeing with the aims of vegetarianism for aesthetic and moral reasons, it is my view that a vegetarian manner of living by its purely physical effect on the human temperament would most beneficially influence the lot of mankind.

> **TEACHING A CHILD NOT TO STEP ON A CATERPILLAR IS AS VALUABLE TO THE CHILD AS IT IS TO THE CATERPILLAR.**
> —BRADLEY MILLAR

Vegetarians have excelled as world-class athletes, dispelling the myth that meat is needed for strength, stamina, and athletic prowess. Olympic swimmer Johnny Weissmuller, the actor who played Tarzan in the movies, was a vegetarian. Nine-time Olympic gold medal winner sprinter Carl Lewis was and still is a vegetarian. In his prime, Lewis earned the nickname "the fastest man alive." Two-time gold medal winner Edwin Moses, who is considered the greatest track-and-field hurdler of all time and never lost a race from 1977 to 1987, is also a vegetarian.

On a musical note, classical violinist Yehudi Menuhin was a vegetarian before he died, and Indian sitarist and composer Ravi Shankar and pop superstar Sir Paul McCartney are vegetarians. The founder of Apple Computer, billionaire Steve Jobs, has been a vegetarian for decades. Henry Ford, creator of the first automobile assembly line and the first vegetable-oil-powered motorized vehicle, was a vegetarian. Greek philosopher Epicurus (undoubtedly the first epicurean) was a vegetarian. Nobel Prize recipient Isaac Bashevis Singer passionately wrote:

> To be a vegetarian is to disagree—to disagree with the course of things today. Starvation, world hunger, cruelty, waste, wars—we must make a statement against these things. Vegetarianism is my statement.

> WE ALL LOVE ANIMALS. WHY DO WE CALL
> SOME "PETS" AND OTHERS "DINNER"?
> —K.D. LANG

Many of history's great spiritual personages were vegetarians and taught vegetarianism, though their present-day religious followers may not follow their example. To name a few: Avatar Krishna of Hinduism, Siddhartha Gautama—the Buddha, Mahavir of Jainism, Guru Nanak Dev of Sikhism, the great poet-saint Kabir Sahib (revered by both Muslims and Hindus), and others. According to testimony by some of his contemporaries, the Prophet Muhammad enjoyed excellent health on a simple diet consisting primarily of dates, barley, and camel's milk. We shall later explore compelling evidence that suggests Jesus Christ and most of his early followers were also vegetarians.

African American Vegetarians

Civil rights leader Coretta Scott King, author Alice Walker, comedian and social activist Dick Gregory, hip-hop entrepreneur Russell Simmons, actress Angela Bassett, and Miss Black USA Elizabeth Muto are only a few of the many African Americans who have adopted compassionate, vegetarian diets. They advocate a world in which all species and people are treated with dignity.

> The animals of the world exist for their own reasons. They were not made for humans . . .
>
> As a woman of African descent, I can easily compare the treatment of our ancestors in this country to the way farm animals are treated. These innocent creatures, which have the right to live and enjoy life, are bred for slavery and slaughter. They have every right to live free, just like all things that live on this earth.
>
> —ALICE WALKER, ACTIVIST, PHILOSOPHER, AND AUTHOR OF *THE COLOR PURPLE*

Many African Americans promote plant-based diets as a response to the widespread chronic health problems faced by the black community, including high blood pressure, heart disease, obesity, cancer, and diabetes. According to the Centers for Disease Control and Prevention, half of all black women and more than a quarter of all black men are obese. Prostate and breast cancer strike almost 40 percent of black men and more than 30 percent of black women, respectively. And one in four black women over the age of fifty-five has diabetes.

Coretta Scott King, wife of the late Dr. Martin Luther King Jr., called her adoption of a vegetarian diet in 1995 a blessing. Her son, Dexter, has been a vegetarian since 1988, and he said that an appreciation for animal rights is the logical extension of his father's philosophy of nonviolence (and, arguably, the single greatest moral influence on Dr. King was vegetarian and pacifist Mahatma Gandhi).

> MARTIN LUTHER KING JR. TAUGHT US ALL
> NONVIOLENCE. I WAS TOLD TO EXTEND
> NONVIOLENCE TO THE MOTHER AND HER CALF.
> —DICK GREGORY, COMEDIAN AND SOCIAL ACTIVIST

Amerindian Vegetarians

When the first settlers arrived in America, they found most native Indian tribes enjoying an abundant and varied diet of vegetables, nuts, fruits, fish, and game. The Choctaw Indians, for example, were known to be especially skillful farmers and subsisted to a large extent on the products of their fields. In addition to several varieties of corn and beans, they cultivated leeks, garlic, cabbage, sweet potatoes, and other garden plants.

Rita Laws, PhD, who is Choctaw and Cherokee, is a scholar and writer in Oklahoma. Her Choctaw name, Hina Hanta, means Bright Path of Peace—and that's what she considers vegetarianism to be. In "Native Americans and Vegetarianism," she wrote:

> Among my own people, the Choctaw Indians of Mississippi and Oklahoma, vegetables are the traditional diet mainstay. A French manuscript of the eighteenth century describes the Choctaw's vegetarian leanings in shelter and food. The homes were constructed not of skins, but of wood, mud, bark and cane. The principal food, eaten daily from earthen pots, was a vegetarian stew containing corn, pumpkin and beans. The bread was made from corn and acorns. Other common favorites were roasted corn and corn porridge . . .
>
> Many history textbooks tell the story of Squanto, a Pawtuxent Indian who lived in the early 1600s. Squanto is famous for having saved the Pilgrims from starvation. He showed them how to gather wilderness foods and how to plant corn.

The Dangers of Animal Food Consumption

Howard Lyman, former fourth-generation farmer and cattle rancher and present-day vegetarian activist, describes how animal-based growers skirt food safety policies at the expense of the consumer.

When a chemical is banned from use, a farmer or livestock operator who has the chemical in stock has a choice: either to lose money by disposing of the product, or to use it and take the risk of getting caught breaking the law. How severe is that risk? Well, if you use a banned product in your cattle feed, you have to face the prospect that the government is going to inspect one out of every 250,000 carcasses. They will test this carcass not for all banned substances, but just for a small fraction of them. And even if they detect some residue of a banned substance, and even if they're able to trace the carcass to the ranch that produced it, the guilty rancher is likely at most to receive a stern letter with a strongly worded warning. I never met a rancher who suffered in any way from breaking any regulation meant to protect the safety of our meat. The whole procedure is, in short, a charade.

In 1991, pathogen control inspector Brian Shelton revealed:

I would expect an extremely high percentage of the chickens would test positive [for contaminants like salmonella and campylobacter]. Our poultry industry clients would not like that.

Injecting hormones into animals is a profit-enhancing practice that speeds growth and puts extra pounds on animals. It has been widely documented that many beef products that reach the market contain estrogenic hormones and residues of antibiotics. Estrogenic hormones cause breast growth in men and contribute to a higher incidence of cancer in women. Antibiotics acquired "secondhand" from eating meat kill beneficial bacteria in the gastrointestinal tract and may reduce the effectiveness of antibiotics in a process called "antibiotic resistance." There is a conspiracy of silence when it comes to infectious pathogens present in beef, pork, and fowl. Animal food inspector William Freeman broke this silence when he went on record saying:

> The oath I took as an inspector said if I ever saw anything wrong I was supposed to report it. But today I can't report anything. Today, if you blow your whistle you're in trouble with the inspection service. I feel the oath I took is violated every day I work.

The full extent of the cover-up is unknown, but the European Union, the United Kingdom, and Japan all have an "on again, off again" relationship when it comes to accepting US-raised animal foods for sale in their countries.

Another problem is deadly "mad cow disease" (bovine spongiform encephalopathy), which is called variant Creutzfeldt-Jakob disease when contracted by humans. When humans eat an animal infected with mad cow disease, they die a hideous death: Their brains are literally liquefied into an amorphous mush by an as yet unstoppable pathogen. This gruesome disease has been traced to the now outlawed practice of feeding herbivorous cows meal containing the brains, fecal matter, feathers, and other body parts of cows, sheep, and birds. Public health officials are alarmed because prions, the infectious proteins that spread the disease, cannot be destroyed even with high heat. This puts the meat-consuming populace at the mercy of profit-seeking factory farmers whose practices are frequently dictated by their ability to save on the cost of all-grain feed rather than the health of the animal or the end consumer.

> IF YOU STEP BACK AND LOOK AT THE DATA, THE OPTIMUM AMOUNT OF RED MEAT YOU EAT SHOULD BE ZERO. —WALTER WILLETT, MD

Every time I pass the fresh meat aisle at the grocery store, my soul stirs a little, thinking of the lives lost.
—RIMJHIM DUGGAL, MD

2.
The Health
Benefits
of a
Vegetarian
Diet

The US Centers for Disease Control and Prevention estimates that 70 percent of all disease is diet-related. Epidemiologically, a well-balanced vegetarian diet has been shown to statistically increase longevity and reduce the overall incidence of degenerative disease. Being a vegetarian, however, brings with it no health guarantee: There are sick vegetarians who overeat, consume too many nutritionless foods, and don't eat enough health-protective fruits and vegetables. If a vegetarian who is hypothetically doing "everything right" in the diet department still gets sick, one ought not blame the imagined inadequacies of the vegetarian diet, but rather consider his or her illness the result of an unfortunate combination of factors: the effects of genetics, stress, environmental pollution, karmic destiny, or some other unknown factor.

Dispelling Lingering Myths

In the 1800s, vegetarianism trickled into North America along with Asian transcendentalism and the European "nature cure" movement. In "meat and potatoes" America, abstaining from animal foods was initially perceived as fringe and dangerous. An exception to the norm was an early American pioneer, the gentle vegetarian Jonathan Chapman (better known as Johnny Appleseed), who chose not to eat the flesh of his friends the animals and was revered and protected by his native admirers.

Without setting out to do so, thousands of scientific studies have legitimized vegetarianism as a diet with far fewer health risks compared with a diet that includes animal foods. In the United States alone, the health cost of meat consumption is estimated to be up to $60 billion a year due to the higher prevalence of hypertension, heart disease, cancer, type 2 diabetes, gallstones, obesity, and food-borne illness among omnivores as compared with vegetarians.

In spite of these sobering, revealing statistics, there are still those who doubt the nutritional adequacy of the vegetarian diet. We will herewith dispel the most common myths.

Getting Enough Protein

The argument that one needs to eat animal foods to receive sufficient protein is perhaps the biggest nutritional myth. According to the American Dietetic Association's 2009 position paper on vegetarian diets:

> It is the position of the American Dietetic Association that appropriately planned vegetarian diets, including total vegetarian or vegan diets, are healthful, nutritionally adequate, and may provide health benefits in the prevention and treatment of certain diseases.

It is not true that vegetarians have a harder time meeting their protein needs. Highly absorbable protein is plentiful in the vegetable kingdom as long as one eats sufficient calories derived from whole, unprocessed foods. What's more, actual protein needs per day are appreciably less than is generally thought. Daily protein intake has been set artificially high by biased medical experts hired by the meat lobby, who have in turn influenced governmental recommendations in favor of higher protein intake. The World Health Organization recommends only 25 grams of protein per day. The American Meat Board recommends 75 grams, contributing to excess protein consumption, which is linked to increased incidence of degenerative disease.

Amino acids make up proteins, and those derived from plant foods have the same biological value as meat-sourced amino acids. Amino acids are amino acids, no matter where they come from. For several decades it was erroneously taught that it was necessary to eat a combination of foods made up of the nine essential amino acids at one meal (e.g., combining rice with beans or nuts with dairy). We now know that this is not necessary, as our bodies have an amino acid pool that combines amino acids derived from previous meals to make complete proteins. As long as one eats enough calories drawn from whole plant foods, getting enough protein from a vegetarian diet will not be an issue.

While we're on the subject of protein, those who eat meat as their primary source of protein typically consume unhealthy amounts of saturated fat and dietary cholesterol. High saturated fat and cholesterol intakes have been definitively identified as primary risk factors for cardiovascular disease, the number one killer in modern societies worldwide. Compared with meat eaters, lifelong vegetarians have a 24 percent lower incidence of coronary heart disease—and vegans have a 57 percent lower rate! There is only one source of dietary cholesterol: animal foods.

> Vegetarians always ask about getting enough protein.
> But I don't know any nutrition expert who can plan a
> diet of natural foods resulting in a protein deficiency,
> so long as you're not deficient in calories. You need only
> five or six percent of total calories in protein . . . and it
> is practically impossible to get below nine percent in
> ordinary diets.
>
> —NATHAN PRITIKIN

Getting Enough Calcium

Vegetarians and vegans have a significantly lower incidence of osteoporosis than meat eaters even though they generally consume less bone-supporting calcium. Those who eat meat-centered diets need to consume more calcium than those who eat plant-based diets because the excess acidity produced by animal foods requires more alkaline-forming calcium to buffer the bloodstream from this acid onslaught. It is not difficult for vegetarians to get enough calcium to meet their daily needs if they eat enough calcium-rich foods, such as leafy greens, broccoli, almonds, carrots, sesame seeds, etc.

Getting Enough Vitamin B_{12}

Harvard University's Frederick Stare, PhD, who died in 2002 but was arguably the world's foremost B_{12} authority, said there's only one source of B_{12}—the beneficial microorganisms that synthesize B_{12} themselves. These grow on plants; in animals; and in our own intestines and nasal cavities, and even between our gums and teeth. Vegetarians and nonvegetarians alike need to find reliable external sources of human-active vitamin B_{12} to supplement internal production. Nonhuman-active "analog" forms of B_{12} are plentiful in nature; they are found in some foods (e.g., spirulina) but cannot be absorbed by humans. The actual amount of B_{12} we need to consume daily is minuscule, measured in micrograms, which is one-millionth of a gram. The average daily requirement is between only 0.01 and 0.03 micrograms. There are people who constitutionally need higher daily doses, especially those who live unhealthy lifestyles or are taking drugs, whether pharmaceutical or recreational. For these people—and any vegetarians and vegans who want "nutritional insurance," B_{12} supplements are readily available in most health food stores; licensed health professionals also administer B_{12} shots.

Although it is a common misconception that vegetarians and vegans have a higher incidence of vitamin B_{12} deficiency than the general population, it has never in fact been shown to be the case.

> Some people are still going to want to eat meat. [The American Meat Institute does] agree, though, that vegetarianism is a healthier diet.
> —DAVID STROUD

Of the few cases in which B_{12} deficiency was found in a vegetarian/vegan, other health factors were always present that were thought to be responsible for pulling down B_{12} levels. The underlying problem in these cases is usually not with B_{12} supply, but rather with the inability to utilize what is consumed or the lack of internal production by beneficial bacteria, which occurs when antibiotics are overused. This does not mean vegetarians and vegans can be cavalier about B_{12} intake, because the quality of the food supply is not what it used to be.

In a more natural, simpler world, eating fresh garden produce would make the B_{12} deficiency problem a nonissue, as more than 70 percent of soil microorganisms produce active B_{12}. Nowadays, however, conventional produce, and even organic produce, is often overly washed, and most of the B_{12}-producing beneficial bacteria are washed away as well. Eating an animal product carries no guarantee of getting any B_{12} either, and with the health risks associated with meat eating, it's a bad idea at best.

A simple solution to the B_{12} issue is to eat foods that have been enriched with B_{12} by the manufacturers. Nutritional yeast, certain breads, and soy milk are examples of B_{12}-enriched foods. Taking a B_{12} supplement is an option, of course. Sometimes B_{12} is included in multivitamin formulations, but it is believed that assimilation is greatly improved if a "stand-alone" B_{12} formula is used, either sublingually (dissolved under the tongue) or as a nasal spray.

Human Physiology: Is It Wise to Eat Meat?

Although humans are indeed capable of digesting meat, health statistics clearly favor a diet of plant foods. Just because we can eat meat, should we?

According to paleontologists, the earliest humans came from equatorial Africa. Northward migration and successive ice ages created human groups like the Eskimos who were forced to adapt to cold, hostile environments where fresh vegetation was scarce or nonexistent. Arctic Eskimos are living proof that humans can survive on a nearly all-meat diet. Does this mean the rest of humanity can eat meat with impunity? Health statistics say no, given the proven health risks associated with meat eating.

> Nothing will benefit human health and increase chances for survival of life on Earth as much as the evolution to a vegetarian diet.
>
> —ALBERT EINSTEIN

Over the millennia, the Eskimos' anatomy and physiology have undergone at least some adaptation as a response to the effects of harsh climate and forced abstinence from plant foods. Eskimos are able to gulp down large chunks of raw, blubbery meat and digest it. In fact, the word "Eskimo" means "those who eat it raw." They can accomplish this because hydrochloric acid, the digestive juice that helps break down protein, is secreted in much greater quantities in Eskimos than in other humans.

Although human beings can and do eat meat, our digestive apparatus and anatomical structures are vastly dissimilar to those of both carnivores (e.g., lions and tigers) and herbivores (cows and sheep). We most resemble bonobos, a small species related to chimpanzees, who eat mostly fruits and other vegetation. Nevertheless, because of the wide

range of foods some humans do eat, scientists consider us omnivores. Other researchers make the distinction of classifying humans as behavioral omnivores, not true omnivores, because humans suffer negative health consequences when we exercise our omnivorous adaptive capability. Bears, dogs, and pigs are classified as true omnivores, and for this reason they do not suffer higher rates of heart disease, cancer, type 2 diabetes, and osteoporosis when they eat meat.

> EXCESSIVE ANIMAL PROTEIN IS AT
> THE CORE OF MANY CHRONIC DISEASES.
> —T. COLIN CAMPBELL, PHD

Formal Studies

Since 1954, in cooperation with the National Institutes of Health, the National Cancer Institute and Loma Linda University have published more than 250 articles in scientific journals on the superior health of the largely vegetarian Christian sect the Seventh-Day Adventists (SDAs) compared with that of the general US population.

SDAs do not drink alcohol or smoke tobacco, and most are vegetarian, though some are not, giving researchers the opportunity to measure the differences in health status between vegetarian and nonvegetarian members. Scientists found that SDA vegetarian men live an average of more than three years longer than Adventist men who eat meat. According to Winston Craig, PhD, of the Seventh-Day Adventist Andrews University in Berrien Springs, Michigan:

> Adventists, in general, have 50 percent less risk of heart disease, certain types of cancers, strokes, and diabetes. More specifically, recent data suggests that vegetarian

men under 40 can expect to live more than eight years longer and women more than seven years longer than the general population.

Vegetarians have the best diet. They have the lowest rates of coronary disease of any group in the country. Some people scoff at vegetarians, but they have a fraction of our heart attack rate and they only have 40 percent of our cancer rate. They outlive other men by about eight years now.

—WILLIAM CASTELLI, MD

Researchers believe these added years of life and better quality of health are due to the protective influences of more fruits, vegetables, and whole grains as well as the abstinence from most animal-derived foods, tobacco, and alcohol.

A study published in the *International Journal of Cancer* concluded that red meat is strongly associated with breast cancer. The National Cancer Institute says that women who eat meat every day are nearly four times more likely to get breast cancer than those who do not eat meat. In contrast, women who consume at least one serving of vegetables a day reduce their risk of breast cancer by 20 to 30 percent, according to the Harvard Nurses' Health Study. Studies done at the German Cancer Research Center in Heidelberg suggest that the immune systems of vegetarians are more effective in killing off tumor cells than those of meat eaters are and that a plant-based diet also helps protect against prostate, colon, and skin cancers.

> I DON'T UNDERSTAND WHY ASKING PEOPLE TO EAT A WELL-BALANCED VEGETARIAN DIET IS CONSIDERED DRASTIC, WHILE IT IS MEDICALLY CONSERVATIVE TO CUT PEOPLE OPEN AND PUT THEM ON CHOLESTEROL-LOWERING DRUGS FOR THE REST OF THEIR LIVES.
> —DEAN ORNISH, MD

Official Recognition by Health Authorities

The American Dietetic Association states that a well-balanced vegetarian diet not only is nutritionally adequate, but also provides more protection from chronic diseases than diets that include animal foods. Andrews University's Craig says:

> In 1992, the U.S. Department of Agriculture unveiled its Food Guide Pyramid in which the bulk of the diet was to be plant based. The pyramid suggested an intake of 11–20 servings daily from breads, cereals, pasta, rice, fruits, and vegetables.

In 1993, the [Seventh-Day Adventist] General Conference Nutrition Council adapted the US Department of Agriculture's pyramid for a vegetarian dietary approach. In 1995 the US Department of Agriculture and the US Department of Health and Human Services stated for the first time that "vegetarian diets are consistent with the dietary guidelines for Americans and can meet the [recommended daily intakes] for nutrients."

The Vegetarian Food Pyramid

Use the Vegetarian Food Pyramid to build a healthy diet. How many servings you should eat per day is based on how many calories you burn. If you don't get much exercise, eat a lower number of servings, such as six servings of grains. If you're very active, you can eat a higher number of servings.

FOOD GROUP	SERVINGS	SERVING SIZE
Grains	6–11	• 1 slice bread • ½ cup cooked rice, cereal, or pasta • 1 cup dried cereal
Fruits and Vegetables	3–5	• 1 cup raw • ½ cup cooked
Dairy or Alternatives	2–4	• 1 cup milk or equivalent • 1 cup cottage cheese • ¾ cup low-fat yogurt
Legumes, Nuts, Seeds	2–4	• ½ cup cooked dried beans or peas • 1 ounce tofu • ¼ cup nuts or seeds • 2 tablespoons nut butter

Source: *Winston Craig, "The Vegetarian Diet," www.vegetarian-nutrition.info/positions/ english/vegetarian_diet.php*

3.
The Ethics
of a
Vegetarian
Diet

Ethics is the study of the standards of human conduct; its application in everyday life is morality. Ethics help us distinguish why certain acts are "right" or "wrong." Our complex legal codes and the punishments meted out for various crimes are based on underlying ethical/moral principles. One may ask, What do animals, whose intellects are undeveloped, know about human ethics and morality? And if animals themselves cannot live by an ethical code or live "moral" lives, do animals have basic rights, such as the right not to be eaten as food by humans?

Nobel Peace Prize recipient His Holiness the Dalai Lama offered an answer to the question of the basic rights of animals in his statement to the Nineteenth World Vegetarian Congress in 1967.

I do not see any reason why animals should be slaughtered to serve as human diet when there are so many substitutes. After all, man can live without meat. It is only some carnivorous animals that have to subsist on flesh. Killing animals for sport, for pleasure, for adventures and for hides and furs is a phenomenon which is at once disgusting and distressing. There is no justification in indulging in such acts of brutality.

In our approach to life, be it pragmatic or otherwise, the ultimate truth that confronts us squarely and unmistakably is the desire for peace, security and happiness. Different forms of life in different aspects of existence make up the teeming denizens of this earth of ours. And, no matter whether they belong to the higher group as human beings or to the lower group, the animals, all beings primarily seek peace, comfort and security. Life is as dear to a mute creature as it is to a man. Just as one wants happiness and fears pain, just as one wants to live and not to die, so do other creatures.

> I AM IN FAVOR OF ANIMAL RIGHTS
> AS WELL AS HUMAN RIGHTS. THAT IS THE WAY
> OF A WHOLE HUMAN BEING.
> —ABRAHAM LINCOLN

For someone raised in a meat-eating family, eating animal foods may have been part of the family tradition for centuries and may also feel right. To that person, meat tastes good, smells good, and makes him or her feel good. Yet something having been common practice over time or feeling good does not constitute valid justification for the ethical merit of an action. If this were so, human slavery, the unequal treatment of women, even cannibalism would be acceptable in some societies on the grounds of "tradition."

> We can see the multiple benefits of vegetarianism. Whether one tries this diet for physical health, for improved intellect and mental well-being, or for spiritual growth, one finds benefits.
> —SANT RAJINDER SINGH JI MAHARAJ

> The more we learn of the true nature of non-human animals, especially those with complex brains and corresponding complex social behavior, the more ethical concerns are raised regarding their use in the service of man—whether this be in entertainment, as "pets," for food, in research laboratories, or any of the other uses to which we subject them.
> —JANE GOODALL, PRIMATOLOGIST, ENVIRONMENTALIST, AND ETHICAL VEGETARIAN

The "right" or "wrong" of eating meat cannot be based on mere personal preference unless one holds the equally questionable ethical stance that "might makes right"—that the stronger should be able to use the weaker however they please simply because they are more powerful. Such logic would support the euthanasia of infants with birth defects, the senile, the comatose, and the infirm—there would be no basis for the protection of the helpless or for those who do not "contribute" to society. We would live out our lives in fear of death, knowing that the life spans of our loved ones and ourselves could be cut short at any time.

Not all human societies share the same moral codes, yet the injunctions "Thou shalt not kill," "Thou shalt not steal," and "Thou shalt not lie" approach universality in their acceptance as ethical ideals.

> NON-VIOLENCE LEADS TO THE HIGHEST ETHICS,
> WHICH IS THE GOAL OF ALL EVOLUTION.
> UNTIL WE STOP HARMING ALL OTHER LIVING
> BEINGS, WE ARE STILL SAVAGES.
> —THOMAS A. EDISON

While those who seek to justify eating animals on ethical grounds may invoke some "special case" hierarchy of competing ethical values, ultimately what makes eating animals morally indefensible is the principle that it is inherently wrong to inflict unnecessary suffering on a sentient, feeling living creature. Let's explore this word "unnecessary," because it is key to our discussion. It is necessary for a lion or another carnivore to kill a zebra for food, for it knows no other way to survive, being programmed by instinct. In the case of humans, we can eat from the vegetable kingdom and not only survive but thrive, making eating animals unnecessary.

Vegetarianism and Karma

I died as mineral and became a plant.
I died as plant and turned to animal.
I died as animal and became human.
What fear I, then, as I cannot diminish by dying?

—JALALUDDIN RUMI

The moral, ethical, and spiritual edifice upon which vegetarianism stands is connected to the principle of ahimsa, a Sanskrit word describing a way of living based on nonviolence in thought, word, and deed. Our food comes onto our plates by some means. According to the law of karma, the violence involved will require recompense in the future. The law of cause and effect requires payment in kind for every action and thought. Whether we kill the animal ourselves or by proxy by allowing a butcher to do the deed, we share the responsibility. American transcendentalist Ralph Waldo Emerson alluded to this in his book *The Conduct of Life.*

> You have just dined, and however scrupulously the slaughterhouse is concealed in the graceful distance of miles, there is complicity.

To live by the principle of ahimsa is important not only for the sake of animals, but also for our own spiritual welfare. According to many spiritual traditions, a heavy karmic debt is accrued if one fails to live a nonviolent life. This weighs down the soul to such a degree that spiritual progress is slowed; some could lose their hard-earned human status and experience future birth in another form of life. It has been warned that the karmic penalty for taking the life of an animal may be incarnating as an animal that will itself be slaughtered for food. This is Old Testament–style justice, an eye for an eye, a tooth for a tooth, and a life for a life. And so turns the wheel of life! According to some traditions, if we are fortunate enough to meet a master-soul or spiritual master, he or she may have mercy on us, intercede on our

> IF A MAN ASPIRES TOWARDS A RIGHTEOUS LIFE, HIS FIRST ACT OF ABSTINENCE IS FROM INJURY TO ANIMALS.
> —LEO TOLSTOY

behalf by taking over our karmic debts, and save us from the causal effects of previous karmic deeds and misdeeds in this and previous lifetimes. In one of his verses, the medieval master, weaver, and poet Kabir Sahib (1398–1518), known for his direct, often blunt style, exclaimed:

> One advocates quick killing
> And another, slow;
> From both, mercy takes heels and flees.
> O' brother, both go to the abode of fire.

Kabir also speaks of the potential of a genuine master's spiritual grace and compassion to absolve even the most heinous acts, for the power of mercy flows through the saints.

Those who defend meat eating sometimes use the argument that vegetarians have no qualms about selectively killing those species that suit their own purposes: vegetables and grain-yielding grasses for food, trees to build their houses, etc. Why, then, should meat eaters not be allowed to kill animals, birds, and fish in order to feed human beings, the highest form of creation? Doesn't the Lord in the Jewish and Christian traditions give humans "dominion over" the lower species?

The "selective killing" argument erroneously equates the taking of the life of a mammal, bird, or other animal with the self-evidently lesser sin of uprooting a turnip or harvesting grain. Spiritual adepts tell us there is some karmic penalty involved in the harvesting and eating of plants, but only a contrarian would insist that the snuffing out of the life of an animal, or a child for that matter, is on equal footing with the beheading of carrots and the boiling of potatoes!

Just as Western science categorizes four states of matter (solid, liquid, gas, and plasma), philosopher sages in ancient India symbolically assigned the building blocks of physical creation—what they called the "five elements" (earth, water, fire, air, and ether)—to levels of consciousness possessed by various species of life.

In this way of ordering creation, even stones (the earth element) have a primitive, rudimentary awareness, however dim, but a stone's feeling nature, including its ability to feel suffering, is negligible. Plants (earth and water elements) are more conscious, and indeed, when their leaves or branches are plucked, stress reactions can be electrically recorded on a polygraph machine, as shown in the experimental work of biocommunication pioneer Cleve Backster.

Further climbing up the ladder of creation, fish and reptiles (water and fire elements) and birds (predominantly fire and air elements) are more sentient and therefore suffer more than plants. Higher still are humans and other mammals, who possess fully developed feeling natures (ether element), including strong maternal nurturing behavior that can involve intense emotional suffering, as when a calf and its mother are separated, or when a young child dies in the arms of his or her mother.

Meat eating perpetrates needless pain, torment, and death on highly conscious, responsive beings. Our need for food can be fulfilled by taking the lives of foodstuffs low on the food chain that are less conscious and feeling. According to karmic theory, the consumption of plants results in little karmic consequence, the killing of certain insects and reptiles requires more karmic repayment, and the killing of birds and mammals results in more severe karmic penalties. Taking a human life carries the greatest consequence; it may result in life imprisonment or the death penalty in this lifetime or in a future lifetime. The law of karma dictates that all outstanding karmic debts are transferred to future existences, human or subhuman. Those who cause suffering will suffer; those who serve and uplift others receive their rewards also. To a limited extent, society and its laws reflect this karmic sensibility.

> Everything in the universe is the fruit of a Just Law, the Law of Causality, the Law of Cause and Effect, the Law of Karma.
>
> —*DHAMMAPEDA* OF GAUTAMA BUDDHA

> A DEAD COW OR SHEEP LYING IN THE PASTURE IS RECOGNIZED AS CARRION. THE SAME SORT OF CARCASS DRESSED AND HUNG UP IN A BUTCHER'S STALL PASSES AS FOOD.
> —J. H. KELLOGG, MD

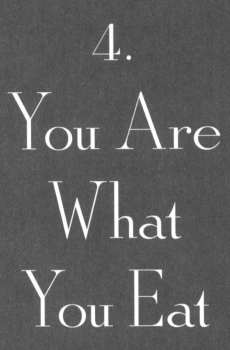

4.

You Are
What
You Eat

In recent years, a tremendous interest in Ayurveda has emerged. Ayurveda, which means "science of life" in Sanskrit, is the traditional medical system of India. It incorporates more than 5,000 years of collective health wisdom. Although it wouldn't be wise to choose an Ayurvedic physician over a well-trained Western surgeon to perform a heart bypass operation, properly trained Ayurvedic doctors have vast knowledge of how to balance the subtle energies governing optimal mind-body functioning. They have a profound understanding of how particular foods affect the body not just from the nutritional standpoint, but also by their effects on our feelings, activities, and inclinations.

According to Ayurveda, foods that are calming, balancing, and energy giving are *sattvic* (Sanskrit for "pure"), because they inherently promote good health and are conducive to spiritual development. In this category are most fruits and vegetables, grains, beans, seeds, nuts, and dairy products (if procured in a compassionate way). From the Ayurvedic perspective, the larger the percentage of sattvic foods eaten, the better, for they are "in the mode of goodness" and promote a healthy society and world.

Meat is considered primarily *rajasic*, or stimulating, agitating, and inflaming, and secondarily *tamasic*, or lethargy producing. Rajasic stimulation often leads to enervation and depressed functioning. Over the millennia, Ayurvedic practitioners observed that if rajasic foods are eaten in sufficient quantity, they inflame the passions and make one prone to lust and aggressive behavior, which, in turn, results in imprisoning, binding actions. Of course, meat eating is not the only cause of hypersexuality, war, and aggression, but meat-centered diets contribute to these imbalanced energies and activities.

How and why do animal foods produce these powerful negative effects? When animal foods are eaten, the body goes into a sort of high-gear, emergency mode: Copious amounts of hydrochloric acid are urgently needed to digest meat, or these carcass remnants will literally putrefy in the intestinal tract (contributing to colon cancer). When this happens, the nervous system experiences significant physiological excitability and arousal, which may be perceived as a sort of pleasurable stimulation. This is why the craving for meat, when it is eaten habitually, is based on more than just taste enjoyment; it is actually tied to a stimulating physiological experience, the addictive power of which should not be underestimated.

Another theory explaining meat's addictive quality points to the powerful adrenal hormones released into an animal's bloodstream and tissues at the time it is killed. Hormone-laced meat is a potent chemical trigger that creates a stimulating response in the consumer. The cost of this to personal health and planetary well-being is astronomical and far outweighs the benefit from any short-lived chemical high.

> STRIVING FOR INNER PEACE REQUIRES LIVING A LIFE OF OUTER PEACE AND NON-VIOLENCE.
> —RIMJHIM DUGGAL, MD

I do feel that spiritual progress does demand at some stage that we should cease to kill our fellow creatures for the satisfaction of our bodily wants.

—MAHATMA GANDHI

Those who were vegetarian by 30 had recorded five IQ points more on average at the age of 10. Researchers said it could explain why people with higher IQ were healthier as a vegetarian diet was linked to lower heart disease and obesity rates.

—BBC NEWS, REPORTING ON AN 8,179-SUBJECT STUDY PUBLISHED IN THE *BRITISH MEDICAL JOURNAL*

Practicing a vegetarian diet is one conscious step towards reducing our carbon footprint, one giant step towards preserving our planet.

—RIMJHIM DUGGAL, MD

Vegetarianism, the World Food System, and the Environment

The American fast food diet and the meat-eating habits
of the wealthy around the world support a world food
system that diverts food resources from the hungry.
A diet higher in whole grains and legumes and lower
in beef and other meat is not just healthier for ourselves
but also contributes to changing the world system that
feeds some people and leaves others hungry. The fact is
that there is enough food in the world for everyone. But
tragically, much of the world's food and land resources
are tied up in producing beef and other livestock—food
for the well off—while millions of children and adults
suffer from malnutrition and starvation.

—WALDEN BELLO, PhD

> TREAT THE EARTH WELL.
> IT WAS NOT GIVEN TO YOU BY YOUR PARENTS.
> IT WAS LOANED TO YOU BY YOUR CHILDREN.
> —ANCIENT PROVERB

Changing from a meat-based to a plant-based diet is the single most powerful act we can undertake to reverse the world's environmental pollution and resource wastage. This might sound like an exaggeration, but it is an assertion grounded in the findings of the United Nations in a study released in 2006.

The United Nations' Food and Agriculture Organization issued a nearly 400-page report entitled *Livestock's Long Shadow* that identified the world's rapidly growing herds of cattle as the greatest threat to the climate, forests, and wildlife. They were also blamed for a host of other environmental problems, from acid rain to the introduction of alien species, from desertification to dead zones in the oceans, from poisoned rivers and drinking water sources to destroyed coral reefs.

The report also surveyed the damage done by sheep, chickens, pigs, and goats. But in almost every case, the

> I GREW UP IN CATTLE COUNTRY.
> THAT'S WHY I BECAME A VEGETARIAN. MEAT
> STINKS—FOR THE ANIMALS, THE ENVIRON-
> MENT, AND YOUR HEALTH. —K.D. LANG

world's 1.5 billion cattle were judged to be most to blame. Livestock are responsible for 18 percent of the greenhouse gases that cause global warming. Their intestinal gas and manure produce more than one-third of the world's emissions of methane, which warms the world twenty times faster than carbon dioxide. And the fuel that's used to produce fertilizer to grow the feed that produces meat and to transport it—and to clear existing vegetation for grazing—produces 9 percent of all emissions of carbon dioxide, the most common greenhouse gas.

The impact of animal-based foods on the environment is as staggering as it is complex. Animal food production directly causes the destruction of tropical rain forests and the extinction of thousands of species that live in these botanical treasure houses; massive water shortages, vast "dead zones" in the open ocean, and pollution of waterways, groundwater, and air; and the exacerbation of human starvation by feeding grain to animals instead of to hungry humans. Roughly one-fifth of the world's land is used for grazing, twice the area used for growing crops. Much of this land provided habitat for indigenous flora and fauna before it was cleared for livestock.

Several decades ago, social scientists in China did a cost-benefit analysis of cattle raising for food and concluded that the beef industry would ruin the country. This is why to this day there are very few large beef cattle operations in China.

The United States nonprofit group the Union of Concerned Scientists has concluded that halving the average US household's meat consumption would reduce food-related land use by 30 percent and water pollution by 24 percent. Meat production requires more water than raising crops. For example, 283 grams (10 ounces) of beef requires eighty-five times more water to produce than the same amount of potatoes. Poor farming practices and erosion destroy land fertility. At a minimum, 75 percent of all US topsoil has been lost to date. Eighty-five percent of this loss is directly related to livestock grazing. In the United States alone, more than 260 million acres of forestland have been cleared to create the cropland used in producing the nation's meat-centered diet. Fifty-five square feet of tropical rain forest are consumed to produce every quarter-pound of rain forest beef. In December 1997, the US Senate Agriculture Committee released a report stating that animals raised for food produce 130 times as much excrement as the entire

US human population, roughly 68,000 pounds per second, all disposed of without the benefit of waste treatment. This makes its way into the groundwater sources from which people drink.

> Whether industrialized societies . . . can cure them-
> selves of their meat addictions may ultimately be a
> greater factor in world health than all the doctors,
> health insurance policies, and drugs put together.
> —T. COLIN CAMPBELL AND THOMAS M. CAMPBELL

The book *The Meat Business* argues that global factory farming could lead to environmental and social devastation. In the next two decades, the problem of how to feed at least 8 billion people while protecting our land, water, air, and wild species will become increasingly urgent. The spread

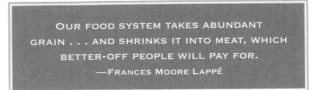

of intensive animal farming throughout the world is not a sustainable solution.

More than 60 percent of Americans and an even higher percentage of Canadians describe themselves as either active environmentalists or sympathetic to conserving the environment. As resources dwindle and awareness grows, the cumulative negative effects of animal-based foods will make the adoption of a primarily plant-based diet more of a social necessity. Not everyone will welcome this change, but such an adjustment will benefit the individual, the planet, and humanity as a whole.

Worldwide, powerful factory farm corporations continue to impose huge tolls on the quality of life for all humans. The 1999 report *Factory Farming and the Environment* from the nonprofit UK group Compassion in World Farming states:

Animal farming is the most environmentally costly way of feeding the world. We have seen that the production of animal protein is a highly inefficient use of land and water resources. Farm animals convert plant protein to animal protein with a low efficiency—typically around 30–40 percent and only 8 percent in the case of beef production. Four kg of grain fed to a pig produces one kg of pork. An estimate from Cornell University is that the water requirement for beef production is over 50 times as much as for rice production and 100 times as much as for wheat production, kilogram for kilogram.

Which action do you think would be more beneficial to the environment: not showering for six months or eliminating just two pounds of meat from your diet over six months? The answer is eliminating the meat: It takes 3,500 gallons of water to shower daily for six months, and 5,000 gallons to produce two pounds of meat.

Let us give thanks to the food.

—Amerindian Prayer

A Word about Organics

What is organically grown food? Is it really better for people and planet? Having studied and practiced regenerative organic gardening and farming for most of my life—long before it became popular—I've been struck by how much better organic produce tastes and makes me feel. Not only are organic grains, vegetables, legumes, fruits, nuts, seeds, and dairy foods produced without petroleum-based fertilizers (which cause massive damage to ecosystems), carcinogenic pesticides and herbicides, hormones, or risky genetically modified organisms, but the organic system also helps preserve and promote biodiversity, closely follows natural cycles, supports family farmers by giving them livable incomes, reduces fossil fuel consumption, efficiently sequesters carbon, and improves soil fertility. If all the arable lands in the world were converted to organic production, the carbon reduction in the atmosphere would be akin to removing 3.5 billion exhaust-spewing cars from the roads! Cutting back on or entirely eliminating meat from the diet in combination with organic agriculture would restore life to our rivers and mitigate the growing dead zones in our oceans. We would reverse the catastrophic consequences of global warming. And our health would improve in the process.

Soil fertility is one of our greatest legacies for posterity, for without good topsoil and sustainable farming practices, our precious planet cannot sustain life as we know it. The nonprofit Rodale Institute provides the results of decades of experimental research and the science to back the claim that not only is organic agriculture more productive and economically viable, but organic foods also contain significantly higher levels of nutrient density and antioxidants than their conventional counterparts—all without the toxic inputs.

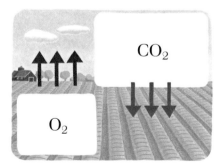

Healthier soil yields healthier, disease-resistant plants. The uptake of beneficial nutrients by plants imparts vigor to those who consume them. One can practice a compassionate diet and gradually incorporate organic foods into it for maximum benefit. I encourage everyone to grow a small organic garden, even if it's only a few planters of tomatoes, salad greens, beans, and peppers on a sunny balcony to start with. We can then better appreciate the cycle of life and where our food comes from.

By sequestering about 1.5 trillion pounds of CO_2 in the soil each year and reducing fossil fuel energy inputs by 50 percent (producing commercial fertilizer requires lots of energy), organic farming could reduce atmospheric CO_2 by 1.1 trillion pounds per year.

Conventional farming adds 925 billion pounds of CO_2 pollutant to the atmosphere each year.

Nutritional Comparisons

According to an exhaustive study by the public Food Standards Agency in the United Kingdom, organic foods had the following higher levels of nutrient density compared with nonorganic foods:

PROTEIN: 12.7 percent

BETA-CAROTENE: 53.6 percent

FLAVONOIDS: 38.4 percent

COPPER: 8.3 percent

MAGNESIUM: 7.1 percent

PHOSPHORUS: 6 percent

POTASSIUM: 2.5 percent

SODIUM: 8.7 percent

SULFUR: 10.5 percent

ZINC: 11.3 percent

PHENOLIC COMPOUNDS: 13.2 percent

Another European Union–funded study that ended in April 2009 involved thirty-one research and university institutes and produced more than 100 scientific papers. According to the UK-based organic-food advocacy group the Soil Association:

> The European Union research program concluded that:
>
> * "Levels of a range of nutritionally desirable compounds (e.g. antioxidants, vitamins, glycosinolates) were shown to be higher in organic crops."
>
> * "Levels of nutritionally undesirable compounds (e.g. mycotoxins, glycoalkaloids, Cadmium and Nickel) were shown to be lower in organic crops."
>
> In addition, levels of fatty acids, such as [conjugated linoleic acid] and omega 3, were between 10-60 percent higher in organic milk and dairy products, and levels of Vitamin C were up to 90 percent higher in leafy vegetables and fruits . . .

In 2006 the European Commission said that "long-term exposure to pesticides can lead to serious disturbances to the immune system, sexual disorders, cancers, sterility, birth defects, damage to the nervous system and genetic damage."

Organic farming and food systems are holistic, and are produced to work with nature rather than to rely on oil-based inputs such as chemical fertilisers, glyphosphate herbicides, and pesticides.

Consumers who purchase organic products are not just buying food which has not been covered in pesticides (the average apple may be sprayed up to 16 times with as many as 30 different pesticides) they are supporting a system that has the highest welfare standards for animals, bans routine use of antibiotics and increases wildlife on farms.

> TO CONSIDER YOURSELF AN ENVIRONMENTALIST AND STILL EAT MEAT IS LIKE SAYING YOU'RE A PHILANTHROPIST WHO DOESN'T GIVE TO CHARITY.
> —HOWARD LYMAN

The Ethics of Tampering with Nature

WHAT ARE GENETICALLY MODIFIED ORGANISMS?

Genetically modified organisms (GMOs) are the products of a relatively new science (commercialized in the 1990s) whose work begins in a laboratory, using genes or fragments of DNA from a variety of foreign animal, virus, microorganism, and plant species. One or more of these DNA segments is "snipped" out and inserted into another plant or animal's DNA in order to create specific characteristics and new species. These characteristics may include giving a

plant the ability to recognize a toxin (such as an herbicide), and the plant can become resistant to that toxin.

This is the case with Monsanto's RoundUp Ready corn, cotton, canola, and soybeans. RoundUp Ready wheat, alfalfa, and rice are awaiting global release, pending regulatory approval. When these GMO crops are planted and the fields are sprayed with the herbicide glyphosate (the active ingredient in Monsanto's RoundUp), the weeds are killed, but not the crop. This is designed to help farmers by making weed control very easy and convenient, but it does not take into account the high toxicity of glyphosate and the untold long-term damage this chemical poison will cause to microorganisms, earthworms, farmworkers, the environment, and consumers. The trillions of microorganisms, earthworms, yeasts, molds, and fungi are part of the web of life and help to promote healthy, fertile topsoil—upon which we and all animals have been dependent since time immemorial.

Another genetic "wonder" is when a trait inserted into the DNA of a plant turns it into a living pesticide. GMO corn is one example of this, into the DNA of which a pesticide-bearing gene from the bacterium *Bacillus thuringiensis* has been inserted. When a corn borer caterpillar, for example, eats any part of the corn plant, it dies from the protein that the transplanted gene produces, because it is toxic to insects of its type. But it is also lethal to monarch butterflies and other beneficial insects.

There has been very little opportunity to really test these GMO products scientifically because they are protected by patents and contracts, preventing independent scientists from exploring their potential dangers and publishing their results without risk of being sued.

BRAVE NEW WORLD

Genetic engineering of seeds is without doubt the most radical transformation in the history of agricultural food production, a history that is more than 10,000 years long. The first GMO product was the Flavr Savr tomato developed by Calgene, a California-based biotech company, which was introduced to the market in 1994. Flavr Savr was a flop, and Monsanto acquired the company.

But other GMO crops were better received. A significant number of GMO crops were developed and sown, primarily in the United States, Argentina, and Canada—most notably soybeans, corn, canola, cotton, and Hawaiian papayas (ever wonder why modern papayas are so uniform in size, shape, and taste?). And these crops, now present in thousands of supermarket foods (but without being identified on the labels), are the dominant crops across the globe. All of this has occurred in an extremely short period of time. StarLink GMO corn, developed by Aventis and approved for use only in animal feed in 1997, resulted in one of the largest FDA food recalls in American history, due to its potential for causing allergies, when it was found in foods produced for humans three years later.

Much of Canada's and the United States' flax crops planted with non-GMO seeds became contaminated with a nasty GMO flaxseed variety called Triffid. It was developed to grow in soil contaminated with herbicides, but was supposedly destroyed when the European Union indicated that it wouldn't permit the sale of GMO crops in its member countries. Triffid flax was deregistered in Canada, and 200 tons of the crop were destroyed. Likewise, almost all of North America's canola crop has been contaminated with GMO varieties, resulting in the loss of hundreds of millions of dollars in export markets that won't accept GMOs.

Organic food production standards prohibit all use of GMO ingredients, along with prohibitions on toxic pesticides, herbicides, chemical fertilizers, sewage sludge, and irradiation. Organic corn and flaxseed were tested and not affected by the StarLink and Triffid recalls.

Choosing organic foods is the consumer's best protection against the dangers of GMOs.

GOOD FOOD IS NOT CHEAP.
CHEAP FOOD IS NOT GOOD. —ADAGE

WILL GMO CROPS END WORLD HUNGER AND HELP SAVE THE FAMILY FARM?

The GMO crops commercialized to date only make the companies who sell them richer, the largest of which is Monsanto, followed by DuPont, AgrEvo, Novartis, and Dow Chemical. Genetically engineered seeds are not developed to make better food, more food, or even cheaper food; they are developed to make a handful of megacorporations more powerful and wealthy by allowing them to control the global seed, herbicide, and pesticide markets. When farmers are sold on the benefits of buying GMO patented seeds, they have to pay significant premiums for the seeds, the prices of which continue to escalate year after year, and then must also buy the pesticides and herbicides that the seeds were developed to resist from the same suppliers. Farmers must sign contracts stipulating that they cannot save their own seeds for replanting the next season, as was the practice for thousands of years. All of this makes for dwindling or non-existent family-farm profits, and the idea that developing countries will be able to solve world hunger and burgeoning populations with GMO crops is naïve and counterintuitive. The result is that tens of thousands of family farmers are losing their traditional farms, which are increasingly being taken over by gigantic factory farms.

DO GMOS INCREASE YIELDS?

As *The Independent*'s environment editor, Geoffrey Lean, reported on April 20, 2008:

> Genetic modification actually cuts the productivity of crops, an authoritative new study shows, undermining repeated claims that a switch to the controversial technology is needed to solve the growing world food crisis.
>
> The study—carried out over the past three years at the University of Kansas in the US grain belt—has found that GM soya produces about 10 per cent less food than its conventional equivalent, contradicting assertions by advocates of the technology that it increases yields.

The most recent landmark research on genetically modified RoundUp Ready soybeans (90 percent of the soybeans
grown in the world are now genetically modified) is entitled
GM Soy: Sustainable? Responsible? and the result of inves-
tigations by an international group of prominent scientists,
scholars, and geneticists. Their research "links GM soy and
Roundup to birth defects, cancer, reproductive problems, and
a host of other health impacts, not to mention environmental
and agronomic impacts."

PLAYING GOD WITH OUR FOOD SUPPLY

Why do we let agriscientists, megacorporations, and gov-
ernments play God with our food supply? The simple
answer is because we, the consuming public, are kept in the
dark about the food industry's dirty little secrets. Genetic
modification of plants and animals raises many ethical and
even theological questions. Does an animal, fish, insect, or
bacterial gene spliced into the DNA of a host plant make
that plant objectionable to vegetarians? Superweeds resistant to ever-increasing amounts of herbicides and rising
rates of cancer and allergies seem to parallel the emergence
and dominance of GMO crops across the globe. Since 1997,

approximately 200,000 farmers in India have committed suicide prompted by crop failures and bankruptcy. The majority of these farmers were traditional cotton growers who switched to GMO cotton. While there may be no proof that this incredibly high suicide rate (one every thirty minutes) is directly related to GMO cotton, some agrarian activists, including the renowned Vandana Shiva, PhD, believe there is a strong correlation.

It is estimated that more than 85 percent of the products in North American supermarkets in 2010 contain some genetically modified ingredients—usually derived from GM soy, corn (high-fructose corn syrup, for example), sugar beets, and canola. Study after study has linked the sustained ingestion of GMO foods to a host of illnesses.

The proverbial genie has been let loose from the lamp. How do we stuff the genie back in and restore the balance? Is it even possible, given the worldwide proliferation of GMO crops? There is no wall high enough to prevent GMO pollen from crossing into an adjoining farm and causing contamination. A fundamental shift can come about only through the efforts of an informed, educated, and politically active public, even if it will take a long time to clean up the environment.

More advocacy by informed politicians who represent constituencies among which this is a growing groundswell will be necessary. Labeling laws must be changed to indicate when a food has been genetically modified, allowing consumers to choose and to know just what it is they are buying and feeding their families. If this sounds radical, it is no more radical than democracy was 200 years ago.

If enough good people unite behind a common noble cause, a tipping point will come about that will force a change and begin to stem the tide. Some understandably don't want to stand out even if they support the principle of avoiding genetically engineered food. Very quietly and discreetly, one can make the individual choice to grow some produce in one's backyard, allocated lot, or balcony and begin to purchase organically grown foods at local stores and farmer's markets. To me, each one of the tens of thousands of organic family farmers is our unsung hero. Without their

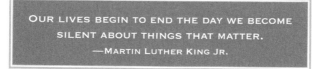

OUR LIVES BEGIN TO END THE DAY WE BECOME
SILENT ABOUT THINGS THAT MATTER.
—MARTIN LUTHER KING JR.

toil and expertise, we would have no food on our plates. As my spiritual mentor, Sant Kirpal Singh, once told me, "To grow a blade of grass is more than a patriot's work." These choices and shifts equate to voting for our health and the health of our planet with our dollars and sense. And this will evolve into a better-informed, healthier, more balanced, and more compassionate world.

5.
Vegetarianism and World Religions

Because all religions emphasize the importance of the qualities of compassion and mercy, it is not surprising that many enlightened beings, prophets, and mystics correspondingly recommend vegetarianism. Unfortunately, over time, original teachings are often diluted, altered, or rationalized away. Krishna, Buddha, Mahavir, Guru Nanak, Kabir Sahib, Jewish prophets, and many early Christian leaders all expounded the vegetarian ideal. Contrary to contemporary popular opinion, early sources indicate that Jesus of Nazareth, who espoused a radically nonviolent way of life, also followed and taught the vegetarian way.

Judaism

Judaism's religious values include the intrinsic worth of human life, the preservation of health, humanity's responsibility as stewards to other living species, and environmental protection of God's beautiful creation. In modern times, the health risks of an animal-based diet and inhumane factory farming practices are in direct conflict with these core principles of Jewish living.

The sixth of the Ten Commandments of Moses states, "Thou shalt not kill" (Exodus 20:13, King James Version). The Hebrew term for "kill"—*lo tirtzach*—refers to killing of any type.

In Genesis 1:29, the first dietary commandment is:

> And God said, "Behold, I have given you every herb-bearing seed which is upon the face of the earth, and every tree, in which is the fruit of a tree-yielding seed; to you it shall be for food."

There is no mention of humans being permitted to eat anything other than plant-based foods.

The story in the Torah about the Great Flood tells us that as a consequence of continuous rain for forty days and nights, every herb-bearing seed and fruit-yielding tree was covered by water! What to do? According to the first chief rabbi of Israel, Abraham Kook, the devastating aftermath of this cataclysm prompted God to grant a temporary moratorium on the original dietary gold standard found in Genesis 1:29, proclaiming that "every moving thing that lives shall be for food" (Genesis 9:3).

According to Rabbi Kook and a growing worldwide Jewish vegetarian movement, permission to eat nonplant foods was meant as a temporary measure only. Humanity, hopefully sooner rather than later, will eventually revert to God's original dietary edict—Genesis 1:29.

Christianity

Like other traditions, Christianity has gone through its epiphanies and trials; it has produced men and women of spiritual realization, some remembered, others forever lost to history. Early Christianity, like Judaism, emphasized both faith and works, and thus guidance was given concerning the treatment of other human beings and animals. The Old Testament and the New Testament both contain passages that unambiguously commend avoiding meat and drink.

> It is good neither to eat flesh, nor to drink wine,
> nor anything whereby thy brother stumbleth, or is
> offended, or is made weak.
>
> —ROMANS 4:21

Jesus lived and taught a path of nonviolence and compassion. While the New Testament Jesus we know today appears to have eaten meat and fish and to have counseled the same, recent scholarship and the earliest Christian manuscripts indicate that vegetarianism played an important role in the early community. The adherents of the earliest forms of Christianity, like those of the Jewish sects from which they emerged, did not eat flesh foods: the Nazarenes, Therapeuts, Ebionites, Gnostics, Essenes, and Montanists were vegetarian. Although English translations of the Gospels mention "meat" on many occasions, all the words used (*broma, brosimos, brosis, prosphagion, trophe,* and *phago*) translate more accurately as "food," "nourishment," or "eating" rather than "meat" or "meat eating" specifically. Regarding the miracle of the loaves and fishes, the earliest Christian manuscripts describe distributing bread and fruit. The loaves and fishes version appeared only after the fourth century; its first appearance is in the Codex Sinaiticus. Important early Christians who supported vegetarianism include Saint Jerome, Tertullian, Saint John Chrysostom, Saint Benedict, Saint Clement of Alexandria, Eusebius, Saint Papias, Saint Cyprian, and Pantaenus.

Recent scholarship supports the view that, prior to the conversion of the emperor Constantine and the push to make Christianity the official religion of the Roman Empire, vegetarianism among many Christian groups was the norm. It was only when Christianity became the official religion of the Roman Empire in the fourth century that a meat-eating

interpretation became the prevailing creed. At the Council of Nicea in 325 CE, politicians and priests altered the text to fit the new orthodoxy. Many changes were made to passages concerned with the eating of flesh and the taking of strong drink to make the new religion more acceptable to the masses. During the reign of Emperor Constantine, vegetarian Christians had to practice their diet in secrecy; if found out, they were put to death for heresy.

The study of early Christianity is fascinating, especially as it applies to the process by which the Bible became what it is today. Christians who believed Jesus had both a human and a divine nature were rendered nearly extinct through persecution.

John Davidson's well-researched *The Gospel of Jesus* presents historical evidence that Jesus, John the Baptist, and many of Jesus's direct disciples, including Peter, Matthew, Thomas, and James the Just (considered by some to be the biological brother of Jesus), belonged to the Nazarene Essene community and were vegetarians who abstained from alcoholic drink. The Essenes were highly revered and considered as healers. Epiphanius of Salamis noted that the Nazarenes:

> Forbid all flesh eating, and do not eat living things at all.
> —*Panarion* 1:1.19.1

> They would not offer sacrifices or eat meat. They considered it unlawful to eat meat or make sacrifices with it.
> —*Panarion* 1:1.18.1

About James the Just, perhaps the biological brother of Jesus, Eusebius wrote, quoting Hegesippus:

> He was holy from his mother's womb; and he drank no wine nor strong drink, nor did he eat flesh.
> —*The History of the Church*

Clement quoted Saint Peter as saying:

> I live on bread alone, with olives, and seldom even with
> pot herbs . . . This is sufficient for me, because my mind
> does not regard things present, but things eternal, and
> therefore no present and visible thing delights me.
>
> —*CLEMENTINE RECOGNITIONS* 7:6

Of the disciple Matthew, Clement of Alexandria wrote:

> Happiness is found in the practice of virtue.
> Accordingly, the Apostle Matthew partook of seeds, and
> nuts and vegetables, without flesh.
>
> —*THE PAEDAGOGUS* 2:1

These early texts indicate that the Twelve Apostles were
vegetarian. *The Clementine Homilies*—written in the
second century and based on the teaching of Saint Peter—
condemn meat eating:

> The unnatural eating of flesh-meats is as polluting as
> the heathen worship of devils, with its sacrifices and its
> impure feasts, through participation in which a man
> becomes a fellow eater with devils.

In *The Gospel of Jesus*, Davidson points out that the eating of meat and the drinking of wine were permitted only later by Paul of Tarsus—a person who never met Jesus in the flesh and therefore was not initiated into the esoteric practices Jesus gave to his direct disciples. After the fourth century, exoteric Christianity blossomed, but by then the daily esoteric practices that increased spiritual receptivity to Jesus's mystical teachings had been essentially lost. Emphasis shifted from the inner life of the spirit to outer rites and rituals, church doctrine, and external authority.

While only a small number of present-day Christian groups recognize vegetarianism as a major tenet of Christian life, some well-known Christian vegetarians of more recent times have been John Wesley of the Methodists, Sylvester Graham of the Presbyterians (and creator of the popular graham cracker), William Metcalfe of the Bible Christian Church, Salvation Army founder General William Booth, and Ellen G. White of the Seventh-Day Adventists. Some contemporary Christian groups that embrace and practice the vegetarian life include the Seventh-Day Adventists; Catholic Concern for Animals; Christians Helping Animals and People; the Universal Christian Gnostic Movement; the

Rosicrucian Fellowship; and the Trappist, Benedictine, and Carthusian monastic orders of the Roman Catholic Church. Many Franciscans are also vegetarian.

In this context, it is interesting that the Doctrine and Covenants of the Mormon Church of Jesus Christ of Latter-Day Saints permits meat eating sparingly, "only in times of winter, or of cold, or famine." By this criterion, except under extreme conditions, virtually no North American Mormon ought to resort to meat eating.

Was Jesus himself a vegetarian? Perhaps the strongest passage affirming this comes from the Essene Gospel of Peace, an Aramaic work written by contemporaries of Jesus that did not make it into the official canon.

> They [asked Jesus]: "Whither should we go, Master, for with you are the words of eternal life? Tell us, what are the sins which we must shun, that we may nevermore see disease?"
>
> Jesus answered: "Be it so according to your faith," and he sat down among them, saying:
>
> "It was said to them of old time, 'Honor thy Heavenly Father and thy Earthly Mother, and do their commandments, that thy days may be long upon the

earth.' And next afterward was given this commandment, 'Thou shalt not kill,' for life is given to all by
God, and that which God has given, let not man take
away. For I tell you truly, from one Mother proceeds all
that lives upon the earth. Therefore, he who kills, kills
his brother. And from him will the Earthly Mother
turn away, and will pluck from him her quickening
breasts . . . And the flesh of slain beasts in his body
will become his own tomb. For I tell you truly, he who
kills, kills himself and whosoever eats the flesh of slain
beasts, eats of the body of death . . . And their death
will become his death . . . That is the path of sufferings,
and it leads unto death. But do the will of God, that his
angels may serve you on the way of life. Obey, therefore,
the words of God: 'Behold, I have given you every herb
bearing seed, which is upon the face of all the earth,
and every tree, in which is the fruit of a tree yielding
seed; to you it shall be for meat . . . Also, the milk of
every thing that moveth and liveth upon earth shall be
meat for you; even as the green herb have I given unto
them, so I give their milk unto you. But flesh, and the
blood which quickens it, shall ye not eat . . .

"For if you eat living food, the same will quicken
you, but if you kill your food, the dead food will kill
you also. For life comes only from life, and from death
comes always death. For everything which kills your
foods, kills your bodies also. And everything which

kills your bodies kills your souls also. And your bodies become what your foods are, even as your spirits, likewise, become what your thoughts are."

—ESSENE GOSPEL OF PEACE, BOOK 1

> I HAVE NO DOUBT THAT IT IS A PART OF THE DESTINY OF THE HUMAN RACE, IN ITS GRADUAL IMPROVEMENT, TO LEAVE OFF EATING ANIMALS.
> —HENRY DAVID THOREAU

As the modern-day poet-saint Sant Darshan Singh Ji Maharaj pointed out in Steven Rosen's *Food for the Spirit*, vegetarianism is wholly consistent with the compassionate life and essential teachings of Jesus Christ.

Jesus Christ was the Apostle of Peace; he was the embodiment of nonviolence. He taught, "Whosoever shall smite thee on thy right cheek, turn to him the other also." [Matthew 5:39] If he was nonviolent to that extent, could he have been violent to the lower rungs of God's creation—the animals, fowl and fish? Christ taught universal love and total nonviolence. He asked us not to indulge in any killing, and he commanded that we have love for all.

Islam

There is not an animal on the earth, nor a creature
flying on two wings, but they are peoples like unto you.

—Quran 6:38

Therewith He causes crops to grow for you, and the olive
and the date palm and grapes and all kinds of fruits. Lo!
Herein is indeed a portent for people who reflect.

—Quran 16:11

Maim not the brute beasts.

—Muhammad

Whoever is kind to the lesser beasts is kind to himself.

—MUHAMMAD

Wild animals and birds were attracted by the spiritual magnetism and love of the renowned eighth-century Muslim saint Rabia al-Basri and would feed from her hand, similar to the way animals flocked to Saint Francis of Assisi. As one story goes, Hasan al-Basri ("from Basra"), a Sufi friend of Rabia's, came to visit her one day. The moment Hasan approached and greeted her, the adoring animals, birds, and butterflies surrounding her scattered in all directions. Somewhat embarrassed, Hasan asked Rabia why the animals ran away when he arrived. Rabia asked, "What did you eat for dinner?" He replied, "Onions and vegetables fried in animal fat." Rabia replied, "You eat their fat and they flee from you."

Our task must be to free ourselves . . . by widening our circle of compassion to embrace all living creatures and the whole of nature and its beauty.

—ALBERT EINSTEIN

Buddhism

Lord Buddha was born into a royal family in Nepal some 2,500 years ago. Leaving a life of luxury, he heroically embarked upon a path of strictest discipline and austerity. After years of extreme penance and meditation, he ultimately attained universal realization and enlightenment. He is known as the Compassionate One, taught the Middle Way, and extended his love to all sentient beings, human and animal. He taught by example and word:

He who, seeking his own happiness, punishes or kills beings who also long for happiness, will not find happiness after death.

—DHAMMAPADA

Because he has pity on every living creature, therefore a man is called "holy."

—DHAMMAPADA

To become vegetarian is to step into the stream which leads to nirvana.

—BUDDHA

NOTHING MORE STRONGLY AROUSES OUR DISGUST THAN CANNIBALISM, YET WE MAKE THE SAME IMPRESSION ON BUDDHISTS AND VEGETARIANS, FOR WE FEED ON BABIES, THOUGH NOT OUR OWN.
—ROBERT LOUIS STEVENSON

Hinduism

The overwhelming majority of the world's Hindus live in India, which has the largest vegetarian population on earth, numbering many millions. Actually, the term "Hindu" is a misnomer, as early invaders named the population of the subcontinent after the Indus River.

Today, "Hindu" means many things to many people, but most commonly is applied to those who follow ancient sages such as the contemplative rishis and yogis, as well as the avatars Rama and Krishna (incarnations of God in the form of the god Vishnu the Preserver). Within the Indian subcontinent, the spectrum of religious thought ranges from strict monotheism (Advaita) to polytheism that includes a sweeping panoply of gods, goddesses, and animist deities.

Vegetarianism is practiced by and supported in the scriptures of the majority of Hindu sects. The most ancient scriptures of India are contained in the Vedas, which are the utterances of rishis and sages. The Bhagavad Gita and the Ram Charit Manas are the most popular scriptures of India.

There are also large Muslim and Christian populations in India, as well as Jews, Jains, Sikhs, Parsis, and Buddhist sects. Many Sufis—adherents to an eclectic and mystical form of Islam—practice vegetarianism and meditation. Amongst the Sikhs, the Namdharis and others on the meditative path follow a lacto-vegetarian diet.

> You must not use your God-given body for killing God's creatures, whether they are human, animal or whatever.
>
> —YAJUR VEDA 12.32

JAINISM

The Jains of India are followers of Mahavira, a Buddha-like sage who lived more than 2,500 years ago. Several million in number, Jains are traditional adherents of Ahimsa and carefully avoid the consumption of meat, fish, fowl, and eggs. *Ahimsa* means kindness and nonviolence toward all living things including animals; it respects living beings as a unity and the interconnectedness of all life.

The greatness of a nation and its moral progress can be judged by the way its animals are treated.

I hold that, the more helpless the creature, the more entitled it is to protection by man from the cruelty of man.

—MAHATMA GANDHI

By not killing any living being, one becomes fit for salvation.

—MANUSMRITI 6:60

The purchaser of flesh performs himsa [violence] by his wealth; he who eats flesh does so by enjoying its taste; the killer does himsa by actually tying and killing the animal. Thus, there are three forms of killing. He who brings flesh or sends for it, he who cuts off the limbs of an animal, and he who purchases, sells, or cooks flesh and eats it—all of these are to be considered meat-eaters.

—MAHABHARATA ANU. 115:40

Vegetarianism was observed in India by the ancient Greek traveler Megasthenes and by Fa-hsien, a Chinese Buddhist monk who traveled there in the fifth century in order to obtain authentic copies of the scriptures.

In the Mahabharata, the great warrior Bheeshma explains to Yudishtira, eldest of the Pandav princes, that the meat of animals is like the flesh of one's own son. Similarly, the Manusmriti declares that one should "refrain from eating all kinds of meat," for such eating involves killing, thus leading to karmic bondage. Elsewhere in Vedic literature, the last of the great Vedic kings, Maharaja Parikshit, is quoted as saying that "the animal-killer cannot relish the message of the Absolute Truth."

> Ahimsa (nonviolence) is the highest dharma. Ahimsa is the best tapas. Ahimsa is the greatest gift. Ahimsa is the highest self-control. Ahimsa is the highest sacrifice. Ahimsa is the highest power. Ahimsa is the highest friend. Ahimsa is the highest truth. Ahimsa is the highest teaching.
>
> —MAHABHARATA 18:116.37–41

He who sees that the Lord of all is ever the same in
all that is—immortal in the field of mortality—he
sees the truth. And when a man sees that the God in
himself is the same God in all that is, he hurts not
himself by hurting others. Then he goes, indeed, to the
highest path.

—BHAGAVAD GITA 13:27—28

High-souled persons who desire beauty, faultlessness
of limbs, long life, understanding, mental and physical
strength, and memory should abstain from acts of
injury.

—MAHABHARATA 18:115.8

Sikhism

Sikhism, one of the youngest world religions, owes its genesis to a lineage of illuminated spiritual teachers known as the Ten Gurus, beginning with Guru Nanak Dev, who lived from 1469 to 1539. The voluminous Sikh scriptures, known as the Adi Granth or the Sri Guru Granth Sahib, were compiled by the fifth teacher in the lineage, Guru Arjan Dev, and discuss a broad spectrum of states of the human condition while singing of the unity and love of one immutable creator.

The Adi Granth is perhaps the only scripture in the world containing compositions by many saints from both the Hindu and Sufi traditions. The largest number of compositions is by Kabir Sahib of Banaras, who was born into a poor Muslim family of weavers. The inclusion of his potent verses and others from members of all social castes demonstrates the universality of the ten gurus.

The gurus placed much emphasis on becoming *khalsa*, or one whose heart is pure and full of light. "Sikh" means "disciple," or "one who learns" (*sishya* in Sanskrit), whereas "guru" means "one who brings light and dispels the darkness of ignorance."

The following advice is found in the Adi Granth:

> By not causing suffering to any living being, you shall go to your True Home with honor.

> O Kabir! Those who consume marijuana, fish and wine—no matter what pilgrimages, fasts and rituals they observe, must pay the price.

> You kill innocent creatures for food, yet call it righteous. Tell me, brother, what do you call unrighteous? *Who is the atheist? Who, the butcher?*

The Sixth Guru, Hargobind, who lived from 1595 to 1644, stated in a letter to disciples:

> Do not even come near meat and fish.

In every age, masters and saints have come to revitalize old, forgotten truths and, perhaps even more importantly, to awaken humanity to its true nature as compassionate, loving beings capable of directly experiencing consciousness of God. The clarion call of the truly enlightened is not to escape from this world into rigid asceticism. Rather, by word and example they teach a higher code of ethics—a global citizenry, if you will, while exhorting students to spend some time daily in meditation practice, learning to rise above the five senses while exploring higher states of mystical union with the divine. For success in this arena, the expert guidance of a living adept is recommended.

Manichaeanism

Mani, a third-century Persian mystic, taught his followers a way to liberate the inner light—which confers enlightenment—that is seen during deep meditation, to free it to return to its source. In Psalm 235 of the Coptic Psalm-Book, he counseled his followers to hew to "the honor of the commandment that we lie not, the honor of the commandment that we kill not, the honor of the commandment that we eat no flesh, the honor of the commandment that we make ourselves pure, the honor of the commandment of blessed poverty, the honor of humility and kindliness."

After the death of Mani, his followers were ruthlessly persecuted in Persia and later by Emperor Justinian. His popular movement was basically rendered extinct.

What Contemporary Spiritual Adepts Say about Vegetarianism

Eating animal foods contributes to the embodied spirit within each human being becoming less receptive to his or her spiritual nature. Sant Kirpal Singh Ji Maharaj was unambiguous about the importance of observing a vegetarian diet. He made the distinction between an ethical life and the inner journey and would often state that "an ethical life is a stepping-stone to spirituality." While living an ethical life is foundational to spiritual experience, it is not in itself spirituality; it is essential to live with care and exactitude in daily life in order to reap the rewards of accurate meditation—the experience of effulgent inner light and the music of the spheres, the highest reaches of which culminate in self-realization and God realization.

In his book *Seven Paths to Perfection*, Sant Kirpal Singh wrote:

A natural diet, comprising vegetables, fruits, nuts, butter, bread and cheese, in moderate quantities, is highly nutritious for the health and strength necessary for carrying on the obligations of life, either earthly or spiritual. An eminent physician says, "We dig our graves in the kitchen, and more deeply with our teeth." Moreover, closely connected with this problem is the far-reaching inexorable Law of Karma—the Law of Cause and Effect, or of Action and Reaction . . . Everything in the world, or of the world, has to be paid for. Even our so-called joys and pleasures require a price. You cannot take away life without paying the penalty thereof.

In *Spiritual Elixir*, he said:

> I wish to say to all aspirants on the Path that it is
> necessary, so long as one is in the physical body,
> that vegetarianism should be strictly adhered to.
> Any relaxation in the matter of diet would not only
> be a definite hindrance in meditation but would
> unnecessarily contract karmic reaction. The real Goal
> is to use every means possible to rise into full God-
> consciousness.

Sant Rajinder Singh Ji Maharaj, the present master in the
same spiritual lineage, writes in "The Vegetarian Diet and
God Realization":

> To be able to concentrate in meditation, we need to be
> calm and collected. If we eat the flesh of dead animals,
> our own consciousness will be affected. We know the
> effect that our own hormones have on our body. Just
> imagine how many stress hormones we are adding
> which were circulating in the animals, birds, or fish
> when they were being killed or slaughtered to be used
> as meat! That is all forming a part of us when we
> partake of it. The food we eat not only has an effect
> upon our physical, emotional, and mental makeup, but

on our spiritual consciousness. If we are trying to lead a life of nonviolence and compassion, if we are trying to become more serene and peaceful, if we are trying to control our mind and senses to concentrate within to find God, then we will naturally want to follow a diet that helps us achieve our goal.

When the Roman poet, Seneca, learned of Pythagoras's teachings, he became a vegetarian. He was glad to discover, to his amazement, that his "mind had grown more alert and more enlightened."

> LET ALL LIVE HUMANELY, FOR EVERY CREATURE SEEKS PEACE IN ITS LIFE. AS WITH HUMANS, ANIMALS ALSO HAVE A HEART BEATING WITHIN THEM; THEIR HEARTS TOO ARE COMPASSIONATE AND FILLED WITH LOVE. CAST A GLANCE OF MERCY SO THAT FROM THE DARKNESS OF INHUMANITY A NEW DAWN BEGINS.
> —DARSHAN SINGH

6.
Concluding
Thoughts

More and more people are turning to the vegetarian way of life. The health benefits alone provide insurance to the individual and his or her family while saving the health care system undue stress and expense. Refraining from consuming the flesh of animals, birds, and fish withdraws support from industries that are in many cases socially, morally, and environmentally reprehensible, while also reducing one's environmental impact. It is also a humanitarian act that supports a shift in the world's food distribution system, which currently leaves millions to starve unnecessarily.

To live more lightly and sustainably on our beautiful planet is to do something tangible and constructive for both present and future generations.

Over the past decades, we have witnessed—at least in North America—many waves of dietary and health trends. One diet or regimen is popular for a few years, only to be replaced by another. While it's true that becoming vegetarian because of the adverse environmental impact of raising animals for food may not in itself lead to a deep and lifelong commitment, we are living in times of growing awareness of the interconnectedness of all life, from both the scientific and spiritual perspectives, and those who connect the humane quality of understanding with the suffering of others—human or animal—are most likely to stay the course, to commit to a life lived from the heart and intelligence of compassion. When a good habit is formed, it becomes second nature. By embracing compassion and evolving to a humane diet, one demonstrates benevolence, not violence, toward the environment and the planet as a whole. This is something we, your authors, have been fortunate to learn and share in both life and work.

Vegetarianism is a life lived from the heart of compassion—for animals, birds, fish, reptiles, the environment, and the planet as a whole. Of course, it embraces members of one's own society, those living in far-off lands, and especially the struggling poor; and it simultaneously demonstrates one's compassion for one's own self, both physically and, more essentially, spiritually. So, we leave the kind reader with these thoughts, hopefully to spark a change for the better in our shared world.

In service,

ARRAN STEPHENS AND ELIOT JAY ROSEN

Never doubt that a small group of thoughtful, committed citizens can change the world. Indeed, it is the only thing that ever has.

—MARGARET MEAD

Resources

❦

Arguments for Vegetarianism

These lists are reproduced with the kind permission of John Robbins, founder of the EarthSave Foundation, from "How to Win an Argument with a Meat-Eater," a poster giving statistics from his book *Diet for a New America*. Please visit EarthSave.org.

The Ethical Argument

- *Number of animals killed for meat per hour in the United States: 660,000*

- *Occupation with highest turnover rate in the United States: slaughterhouse worker*

- *Occupation with highest rate of on-the-job injury in the United States: slaughterhouse worker*

The Hunger Argument

- *Number of people worldwide who will die as a result of malnutrition this year: 20 million*

- *Number of people who could be adequately fed using land freed if Americans reduced their intake of meat by 10 percent: 100 million*

- *Percentage of corn grown in the United States eaten by people: 20*

- *Percentage of corn grown in the United States eaten by livestock: 80*

- *Percentage of oats grown in the United States eaten by livestock: 95*

- *Percentage of protein wasted by cycling grain through livestock: 90*

- *How frequently a child dies as a result of malnutrition: every 2.3 seconds*

- *Pounds of potatoes that can be grown on an acre: 40,000*

- *Pounds of beef produced on an acre: 250*

The Hunger Argument—*continued*

- *Percentage of US farmland devoted to beef production: 56*

- *Pounds of grain and soybeans needed to produce a pound of edible flesh from feedlot beef: 16*

The Environmental Argument

- *Cause of global warming: greenhouse effect*

- *Primary cause of greenhouse effect: carbon dioxide emissions from fossil fuels*

- *Fossil fuels needed to produce meat-centered diet vs. a meat-free diet: 3 times more*

- *Percentage of US topsoil lost to date: 75*

- *Percentage of US topsoil loss directly related to raising livestock: 85*

- *Number of acres of US forest cleared for cropland to produce meat-centered diet: 260 million*

- *Amount of meat imported to United States annually from Central and South America: 300,000,000 pounds*

- *Percentage of Central American children under the age of five who are undernourished: 75*

- *Area of tropical rain forest consumed in every quarter-pound of rain forest beef: 55 square feet*

- *Current rate of species extinction due to destruction of tropical rain forests for meat grazing and other uses: 1,000 per year*

The Survival Argument

- *Athlete to win Ironman Triathlon more than twice: Dave Scott (6-time winner)*

- *Food choice of Dave Scott: vegetarian*

- *Largest meat eater that ever lived:* Tyrannosaurus rex *(Where is he today?)*

The Cancer Argument

- *Increased risk of breast cancer for women who eat meat daily compared to less than once a week: 3.8 times*

- *For women who eat eggs daily compared to once a week: 2.8 times*

- *For women who eat butter and cheese 2 to 4 times a week: 3.25 times*

- *Increased risk of fatal ovarian cancer for women who eat eggs 3 or more times a week vs. less than once a week: 3 times*

- *Increased risk of fatal prostate cancer for men who consume meat, cheese, eggs, and milk daily vs. sparingly or not at all: 3.6 times*

The Cholesterol Argument

- *Number of US medical schools: 125*

- *Number requiring a course in nutrition: 30*

- *Nutrition training received by average US physician during four years in medical school: 2.5 hours*

- *Most common cause of death in the United States: heart attack*

- *How frequently a heart attack kills in the United States: every 45 seconds*

- *Average US man's risk of death from heart attack: 50 percent*

- *Risk of average US man who eats no meat: 15 percent*

- *Risk of average US man who eats no meat, dairy, or eggs: 4 percent*

- *Amount you reduce risk of heart attack if you reduce consumption of meat, dairy, and eggs by 10 percent: 9 percent*

- *Amount you reduce risk of heart attack if you reduce consumption by 50 percent: 45 percent*

The Cholesterol Argument—*continued*

- *Amount you reduce risk if you eliminate meat, dairy, and eggs from your diet: 90 percent*

- *Average cholesterol level of people eating meat-centered diet: 210 mg/dl*

- *Chance of dying from heart disease if you are male and your blood cholesterol level is 210 mg/dl: greater than 50 percent*

The Natural Resources Argument

- *User of more than half of all water used for all purposes in the United States: livestock production*

- *Amount of water used in production of the average cow: sufficient to float a destroyer*

- *Gallons of water needed to produce a pound of wheat: 25*

- *Gallons of water needed to produce a pound of California beef: 5,000*

- *Years the world's known oil reserves would last if every human ate a meat-centered diet: 13*

- *Years they would last if human beings no longer ate meat: 260*

- *Calories of fossil fuel expended to get 1 calorie of protein from beef: 78*

- *To get 1 calorie of protein from soybeans: 2*

- *Percentage of all raw materials (base products of farming, forestry, and mining, including fossil fuels) consumed by United States that is devoted to the production of livestock: 33*

- *Percentage of all raw materials consumed by the United States needed to produce a complete vegetarian diet: 2*

The Antibiotic Argument

- *Percentage of US antibiotics fed to livestock: 55*

- *Percentage of staphylococci infections resistant to penicillin in 1960: 13*

- *Percentage resistant in 1988: 91*

- *Response of European Economic Community to routine feeding of antibiotics to livestock: ban*

- *Response of US meat and pharmaceutical industries to routine feeding of antibiotics to livestock: full and complete support*

The Pesticide Argument

- *Common belief: US Department of Agriculture protects our health through meat inspection*

- *Reality: Fewer than 1 out of every 250,000 slaughtered animals is tested for toxic chemical residues*

- *Percentage of US mothers' milk containing significant levels of DDT: 99*

- *Percentage of US vegetarian mothers' milk containing significant levels of DDT: 8*

- *Contamination of breast milk, due to chlorinated hydrocarbon pesticides in animal products, found in meat-eating mothers vs. non-meat-eating mothers: 35 times higher*

- *Amount of dieldrin ingested by the average breast-fed American infant: 9 times the permissible level*

Selected Sources

Backster, Cleve. "Evidence of a Primary Perception in Plant Life." *International Journal of Parapsychology* 1968;10(4):329–48.

BeDuhn, Jason David. *The Manichaean Body.* Baltimore: Johns Hopkins University Press, 2000.

Cousens, Gabriel. *Conscious Eating.* Santa Rosa, CA: Vision Books International, 1992.

David, Lee. "Why Vegetarianism Is Good for You and the Planet." NewAgeArticles.com. n.d. http://www.newagearticles.com/Article/Why-Vegetarianism-Is-Good-For-You-And-The-Planet/702.

Davidson, John. *The Gospel of Jesus.* Rockport, MA: Element Books, 1995.

The Doctrine and Covenants of the Church of Jesus Christ of Latter-Day Saints, Section 89.12–13. http://scriptures.lds.org/dc/89.

Lean, Geoffrey. "Exposed: The Great GM Crops Myth." *The Independent* April 20, 2008. http://www.independent.co.uk/environment/green-living/exposed-the-great-gm-crops-myth-812179.html.

Pavlina, Erin. *Raising Vegan Children in a Non-Vegan World*. Los Angeles: VegFamily, 2003.

Rosen, Steven. *Food for the Spirit: Vegetarianism and the World Religions*. New York: Bala Books, 1987.

Singer, Peter. *The Life You Can Save*. New York: Random House, 2009.

Smith, Gar. *A Harvest of Heat: Agribusiness and Climate Change*. Agribusiness Action Initiatives—North America, Spring 2010.

Smith, Jeffrey M.. *Seeds of Deception*. Fairfield, IA: Yes Books, 2003.

Soil Association. "Soil Association Response to the Food Standards Agency's Organic Review." July 29, 2009 [press release].

Srimad Bhagavatam 10:1.4.

Swanton, John R.. *Source Material for the Social and Ceremonial Life of the Choctaw Indians*. Washington, DC: United States Government Printing Office, 1931.

About the Authors

ARRAN STEPHENS

Arran Stephens has been at the leading edge of the organic food movement for most of his sixty-seven years. In 1985, he and Ratana, his wife, founded Nature's Path Foods, North America's largest organic breakfast foods company (naturespath.com). Numerous recognitions have come his and Nature's Path's way, amongst them Ernst and Young's Entrepreneur of the Year, Pacific Region, award in 2002; the Canadian Health Food Association Hall of Fame Award in 2005; *Maclean's* magazine's Canada's Best 100 Employers in 2004, 2005, and 2006 and Canada's Top 30 Green Employers in 2009; and the E.F. Schumacher Award, given for attention to sustainability, in 2007. He directs the nonprofit Science of Spirituality Meditation and Ecology Centre in Richmond, British Columbia (sos.org), serves on the board of the Rodale Institute (rodaleinstitute.org), and is the chairman of the Richmond Food Security Society (richmondfoodsecurity.org).

Arran's spiritual memoir, *Journey to the Luminous: Encounters with Spiritual Adepts of Our Time*, was published to acclaim in 1999 and quickly sold out, but it is available gratis on the Web at mothandtheflame.com. His oil paintings have also been widely exhibited. He and Ratana have four children and several grandchildren. He has an enduring commitment to family, community service, sustainability, and spirituality.

ELIOT JAY ROSEN

Coauthor and researcher Eliot Jay Rosen is a health writer, a clinical psychotherapist, and the author of the 1998 *Los Angeles Times* bestseller *Experiencing the Soul*. He has been a vegetarian since 1973.

Eliot's master's thesis, "Health Risk Factors and Policies of the National School Lunch Program," resulted in his authoring four Hawaii State Senate and House bills and influencing school officials to offer more vegetarian alternatives.

Eliot's background includes stints as vegetarian health chef and personal assistant for actor and director Danny DeVito; United Nations speechwriter for the Third International Conference on Health and the Environment; and creator and on-air host of HealthChoice, a Los Angeles–based talk radio show featuring interviews with internationally known nutritional health experts.

Eliot can be contacted at eliotrosen@hotmail.com and through the For a World We Choose Foundation.

All net proceeds from this book will be donated to charities that support a positive, vegetarian lifestyle.

Index

Underscored page references indicate boxed text. **Boldface** references indicate illustrations.